SCIENCE FICTION

This is a volume in the
Arno Press collection

SCIENCE FICTION

ADVISORY EDITORS

R. Reginald

Douglas Menville

See last pages of this volume
for a complete list of titles

THE CHECKLIST

OF

FANTASTIC LITERATURE

IN

PAPERBOUND BOOKS

Edited by

Bradford M. Day

ARNO PRESS

A New York Times Company

New York — 1975

Reprint Edition 1974 by Arno Press Inc.

Reprinted from a copy in the library
of W. R. Cole

SCIENCE FICTION
ISBN for complete set: 0-405-06270-2
See last pages of this volume for titles.

Manufactured in the United States of America

———◆———

Library of Congress Cataloging in Publication Data

Day, Bradford M
    The checklist of fantastic literature in paperbound
books.

    (Science fiction)
    Reprint of the ed. published by Science-Fiction &
Fantasy Publications, Denver, N. Y.
    1. Fantastic fiction--Bibliography. 2. Science
fiction--Bibliography. 3. Bibliography--Paperback
editions. I. Title. II. Series.
[Z5917.F3D33 1975]   016.80883'876   74-15961
ISBN 0-405-06326-1

THE CHECKLIST

OF

FANTASTIC LITERATURE

IN

PAPERBOUND BOOKS

Compiled by

BRADFORD M. DAY

SCIENCE-FICTION & FANTASY PUBLICATIONS

WEHMAN BROS.
Publishers & Distributors
HACKENSACK, N.J., U.S.A.

A listing of paper-covered books with a sufficient tinge of the super-natural, or, the super-scientific as to warrant placement in the science-fantasy field.

The titles under each author have only one edition noted. This is followed by the name of the publisher, year date of publication, and number of pages. The "Book" title is given - when the name of the original hardcover is unchanged, the only notation is: same. The city of publication is not stated in most cases since almost all publishers are located in New York City. The following are exceptions:

  Fawcett (Gold Medal) (Crest) - Greenwich, Connecticut
  Monarch Books - Derby, Connecticut
  Transport Publishing Co. - Sydney, Australia
  Pemberton - Manchester, England
  Arrow Books (Hutchinson) - London
  Badger Books (John Spencer) - London
  Boys' Friend Library - London
  Champion Library - London
  Digit Books - London
  Everybody's Books - London
  Gannet - London
  Hamilton, or, Panther Books - London
  Milestone - London
  Mitre Press - London
  Pan Books - London
  Pharos Books - London
  Scion Ltd. - London
  Edwin Self - London
  Gerald Swan - London
  Utopia Publications - London
  Curtis Warren - London

This checklist is very nearly complete. You will find new titles, and a few old ones that are not included. Additional information will be truly appreciated by the publisher.

Aarons, Edward S.
  ASSIGNMENT TO DISASTER   Fawcett   1955   160
Abbott, Edwin A.
  FLATLAND   Dover   1952   103
Adams, H. C.
  WHEN THE GODS CAME   Badger   nd   158
Aldiss, Brian W.
  GALAXIES LIKE GRAINS OF SAND   Signet   1960   144
  GREYBEARD   Signet   1965   176
  THE LONG AFTERNOON OF EARTH   Signet   1962   192
  NO TIME LIKE TOMORROW   Signet   1959   160
    Book: SPACE, TIME AND NATHANIEL Abr.
  THE PRIMAL URGE   Ballantine   1961   191
  STARSHIP   Signet   1960   160
    Book: same
  BOW DOWN TO NUL   Ace   1960   145
    with Wellman THE DARK DESTROYERS
  VANGUARD FROM ALPHA   Ace   1959   109
    with Bulmer THE CHANGELING WORLDS
Allingham, H. J.
  THE ROBOT MAN   Boys' Friend Library   1931   65
Ambrose, Charles
  MOON MONSTER   Barton   London   nd   32   juv.
Amis, Kingsley and Conquest, Robert (Editors)
  SPECTRUM   Berkley   1963   190
    Book: same Abr.
  SPECTRUM II   Berkley   1964   256
    Book: same
Amper, Drax
  FAR BEYOND THE BLUE   Gannet Press   1953   128
Anderson, Chester and Kurland, Michael
  TEN YEARS TO DOOMSDAY   Pyramid   1964   158
Anderson, Poul
  AFTER DOOMSDAY   Ballantine   1962   128
  BRAIN WAVE   Ballantine   1954   164
    Book: same
  THE ENEMY STARS   Berkley   1958   142
    Book: same
  GUARDIANS OF TIME   Ballantine   1960   140
  THE HIGH CRUSADE   MacFadden-Bartell   1964   160
    Book: same
  ORBIT UNLIMITED   Pyramid   1961   158
  SHIELD   Berkley   1963   158
  STRANGERS FROM EARTH   Ballantine   1961   144
  THREE HEARTS AND THREE LIONS   Avon   1961   160
    Book: same
  THREE WORLDS TO CONQUER   Pyramid   1964   143
  TIME AND STARS   Macfadden-Bartell   1965   176
    Book: same
  VIRGIN PLANET   Beacon   1960   160
    Book: same
  UN-MAN AND OTHER STORIES   Ace   1962   158
    with THE MAKESHIFT ROCKET   Ace   1962   97
  EARTHMAN GO HOME   Ace   1960   110
    with Tucker TO THE TOMBAUGH STATION

Anderson, Poul (Cont.)
    LET THE SPACEMEN BEWARE   Ace   1963   93
      with Bulmer WIZARD OF STARSHIP POSEIDON
    MAYDAY ORBIT   Ace   1961   126
      with Bulmer NO MAN'S WORLD
    NO WORLD OF THEIR OWN   Ace   1955   121
      with Asimov 1000 YEAR PLAN
    PLANET OF NO RETURN   Ace   1957   105
      with Norton STAR GUARD
    STAR WAYS   Ace   1958   143
      Book: same   with Bulmer CITY UNDER THE SEA
    WAR OF THE WING MEN   Ace   1958   160
      with THE SNOWS OF GANYMEDE   Ace   1958   96
    THE WAR OF TWO WORLDS   Ace   1958   108
      with Brunner THRESHOLD OF ETERNITY
    WE CLAIM THESE STARS   Ace   1959   125
      with Silverberg THE PLANET KILLERS
Andrezel, Pierre
    THE ANGELIC AVENGERS   Ace   1962   252
      Book: same
Anonymous
    ACCOUNT OF A RACE OF HUMAN BEINGS WITH TAILS, DISCOVERED BY MR. JONES, THE
      TRAVELER, IN THE INTERIOR OF NEW GUINEA   A T Mason   Melbourne   188-
    THE BLACK CASTLE; OR, THE SPECTRE OF THE FOREST   Dean & Munday   London
      nd (1808)   1 vol.
    HE, A COMPANION TO SHE   Munro   1887   213
    HOW GLASGOW CEASED TO FLOURISH   Wilson & McCormick   Glasgow   1884   64
    "IT." A WILD, WEIRD HISTORY   Munro   1887   242
    THE STORY OF MY DICTATORSHIP   Sterling Pub Co   1894   133
    THE WANDERING SPIRIT; OR, MEMOIRS OF THE HOUSE OF MORNE   no publisher
      London   1802   74
    WHAT MAY HAPPEN IN THE NEXT 90 DAYS   no publisher   1877   33
Anonymous Anthology
    AVON GHOST READER   Avon   1946   258
    AVON MYSTERY STORYTELLER   Avon   1946   257
    AVON STORY TELLER   Avon   1945   283
    THE GIRL WITH THE HUNGRY EYES   Avon   1949   127
    GOTHIC PIECES   no publisher   London   1804   227
    GOTHIC STORIES   Fisher   London   1800   235   Front.
    MORE TALES OF TERROR AND SURPRISE   Mitre Press   nd   127
    A NEW COLLECTION OF GOTHIC STORIES   Fisher   London   1801   276   Front.
    OCCULT: A COLLECTION OF STORIES OF THE SUPERNATURAL   Swan   1945   36
    STRANGE LOVE STORIES   Utopia Pubn   nd   72
    STRANGE TALES   Utopia Pubn   nd   67
    TALES OF MURDER AND MYSTERY   Everybody's Books   nd   50
    TALES OF MYSTERY AND SURPRISE   Everybody's Books   nd   32
    TALES OF TERROR AND THE UNKNOWN   Everybody's Books   nd   96
    TALES OF THE SUPERNATURAL   Pan Books   1947   183
    THRILLING STORIES--ROMANCE, ADVENTURE   Utopia Pubn   nd   36
    THROUGH THE FORBIDDEN GATES AND OTHER TALES   Short Story Pub Co   Boston
      1903   248
    TWENTY-FIVE GREAT GHOST STORIES   Avon   1943   190
Ansky, S.
    THE DYBBUK   Liveright   nd   145
      Book: same

Anstey, F.
   THE BRASS BOTTLE   Penguin   1953   187
      Book: same
Appel, Benjamin
   THE FUNHOUSE   Ballantine   1959   157
Apuleius, Lucius
   THE GOLDEN ASS   Pocket Books   1954   264
      Book: same
Arnold, Edwin L.
   GULLIVER OF MARS   Ace   1964   224
      Book: LIEUT. GULLIVER JONES
Arnold, Frank Edward
   WINGS ACROSS TIME   Pendulum   London   nd   118
Ascher, Eugene
   THE GRIM CARETAKER   Everybody's Books   nd   49
   THERE WERE NO ASPER LADIES   Mitre Press   nd   126
   UNCANNY ADVENTURES   Everybody's Books   nd   49
Ashton, Marvin
   PEOPLE OF ASA   Warren   1953   159
Asimov, Isaac
   THE CAVES OF STEEL   Pyramid   1962   189
      Book: same
   THE CURRENTS OF SPACE   Lancer   1963   191
      Book: same
   EARTH IS ROOM ENOUGH   Bantam   1959   166
      Book: same
   THE END OF ETERNITY   Signet   1958   192
      Book: same
   I, ROBOT   Signet   1956   192
      Book: same
   THE MAN WHO UPSET THE UNIVERSE   Ace   1955   254
      Book: FOUNDATION AND EMPIRE
   THE MARTIAN WAY AND OTHER STORIES   Signey   1957   159
      Book: same
   THE NAKED SUN   Lancer   1964   191
      Book: same
   NINE TOMORROWS   Bantam   1960   198
      Book: same
   PEBBLE IN THE SKY   Bantam   1957   200
      Book: same
   2nd FOUNDATION: GALACTIC EMPIRE   Avon   1958   192
      Book: SECOND FOUNDATION
   THE STARS LIKE DUST   Lancer   1963   192
      Book: same
   1000 YEAR PLAN   Ace   1955   162
      Book: FOUNDATION   with Anderson NO WORLD OF THEIR OWN
   THE REBELLIOUS STARS   Ace   1954   160
      Book: THE STARS LIKE DUST   with Dee AN EARTH GONE MAD
Asimov, Isaac (Editor)
   THE HUGO WINNERS   Avon   1962   320
      Book: same
   MORE SOVIET SCIENCE FICTION   Collier   1962   190
   SOVIET SCIENCE FICTION   Collier   1962   189

Asquith, Cynthia (Editor)
   THE GHOST BOOK   Arrow 1963   287
      Book: same
Atholl, Justin
   THE GREY BEAST Everybody's Books   nd   48
   LAND OF HIDDEN DEATH Everybody's Books   nd   50
   THE MAN WHO TILTED THE EARTH Mitre Press   nd   63
   THE OASIS OF SLEEP Mitre Press   nd   62
Atkins, John (Editor)
   THE NEW SAXON PAMPHLETS: ONE No publisher   nd   48
Author of "Whitefriars"
   THE GOLD WORSHIPPERS, OR THE DAYS WE LIVE IN Harper   1851   236
Aylesworth, John
   FEE, FEI, FO, FUM Avon   1963   158
Ayme, Marcel
   THE GREEN MARE Penguin   1961   237
      Book: same
   THE WALKER THROUGH WALLS Berkley   1962   191
      Book: ACROSS PARIS AND OTHER STORIES

Bahnson, Agnew, Jr.
   THE STARS ARE TOO HIGH Bantam   1960   183
      Book: same
Ballard, J. G.
   BILLENIUM Berkley   1962   159
   THE BURNING WORLD Berkley   1964   160
   THE DROWNED WORLD Berkley   1962   158
   PASSPORT TO ETERNITY Berkley   1963   160
   TERMINAL BEACH Berkley   1964   160
   THE VOICES OF TIME Berkley   1962   158
   THE WIND FROM NOWHERE Berkley   1962   160
Balmer, Edwin and Wylie, Philip
   WHEN WORLDS COLLIDE Paperback Library   1962   192
      Book: same
Banister, Manly
   CONQUEST OF EARTH Airmont   1964   128
      Book: same
Barnard, Allan (Editor)
   CLEOPATRA'S NIGHTS Dell   1950   157
Barr, Tyrone C.
   THE LAST 14 Chariot Books no address   1960   156
Barry, Ray
   BLUE PERIL Warren   1952   128
   DEATH DIMENSION Warren   1951   112
   GAMMA PRODUCT Warren   1952   127
   HUMANOID PUPPETS Warren   1952   127
   OMINOUS FOLLY Warren   1952   112
Bartlett, Landell
   THE VANGUARD OF VENUS Experimenter Pub Co New York   1928   24
Barton, Erle
   THE PLANET SEEKERS Badger   nd   158
   THE UNSEEN Badger   nd   158
Barton, Samuel
   THE BATTLE OF THE SWASH Dillingham   1888   131

Barzman, Ben
  ECHO X   Paperback Library   1962   252
      Book: TWINKLE, TWINKLE LITTLE STAR
Batchellor, John M.
  A STRANGE CONFLICT   Ogilvie   New York and Chicago   1888   299
  A STRANGE PEOPLE   Ogilvie   New York and Chicago   1889   290
Batt, L.
  FORMULA FOR POWER   Pinnacle   Sydney   1941   61
Baum, L. Frank
  THE WIZARD OF OZ   Fawcett   1960   192
      Book: same
Beach, Stewart (Editor)
  THIS WEEK'S STORIES OF MYSTERY AND SUSPENSE   Berkley   1963   190
      Book: same Abr.
Beaumont, Charles
  THE HUNGER, AND OTHER STORIES   Bantam   1959   183
      Book: same
  NIGHT RIDE AND OTHER JOURNEYS   Bantam   1960   184
  YONDER   Bantam   1958   184
Beaumont, Charles (Editor)
  THE FIEND IN YOU   Ballantine   1962   158
Beck, Calvin (Editor)
  THE FRANKENSTEIN READER   Ballantine   1962   159
Belfield, Wedgwood
  PISTOL PAYNE'S JUNGLE SUBMOTANK   Champion Library   1936   64
  WHEN THE WORLD CRASHED   Champion Library   1935   64
Bell, Thornton
  CHAOS   Badger   nd   158
  SPACE TRAP   Badger   nd   158
Bellamy, Francis Rufus
  ATTA   Ace   1954   147
      Book: same   with Leinster THE BRAIN STEALERS
Bengtsson, Frans G.
  THE LONG SHIPS   Signet   1957   414
      Book: same
Bennett, Alfred Gordon
  WHOM THE GODS DESTROY   Pharos Books   London   1946   100
Benoit, Pierre
  ATLANTIDA   Ace   1964   .192
      Book: same
Bonson, D. R. (Editor)
  THE UNKNOWN   Pyramid   1963   192
  THE UNKNOWN FIVE   Pyramid   1964   190
Beresford, J. D.
  NINETEEN IMPRESSIONS   Sidgwick & Jackson   London   1918   226
      Book: same
Beresford, Leslie
  THE FLYING FISH   Boys' Friend Library   1931   65
Berry, Bryan
  AFTERMATH   Hamilton   nd   109
  AND THE STARS REMAIN   Hamilton   1952   112
  DREAD VISITOR   Hamilton   1952   128
  FROM WHAT FAR STAR   Panther   1954   159
      Book: same

Berry, Bryan (Cont.)
    RETURN TO EARTH   Hamilton   nd   111
    THE VENOM SEEKERS   Panther   1954   159
      Book: same
Bester, Alfred
    THE DEMOLISHED MAN   Signet   1954   175
      Book: same
    STARBURST   Signet   1958   160
    THE STARS MY DESTINATION   Signet   1957   197
      Book: TIGER, TIGER
Beynon, John
    STOWAWAY TO MARS   Nova Pubn   London   1953   128
Bidston, Lester
    QUEEN OF THE SKIES   Boys'f Friend Library   1930   64
Bierce, Ambrose
    THE COLLECTED WRITINGS   Citadel   1963   810
      Book: same
    GHOST AND HORROR STORIES   Dover   1964   199
    IN THE MIDST OF LIFE   Signet   1961   254
      Book: same
Biggle, Lloyd, Jr.
    THE ANGRY ESPERS   Ace   1961   136
      with Lowndes THE PUZZLE PLANET
Binder, Eando (Ernest and Otto)
    ADAM LINK IN THE PAST   Whitman Press   Sydney   nd   48
    THE THREE ETERNALS   Whitman Press   Sydney   1950   48
    WHERE ETERNITY ENDS   Whitman Press   Sydney   nd   32
Bingham, Carson
    GORGO   Monarch   1960   141
Bixby, Jerome
    SPACE BY THE TALE   Ballantine   1964   159
Blair, Adrian
    COSMIC CONQUEST   Warren   1953   159
Blake, Stacey
    THE ISLE OF PERIL   Boys' Friend Library   1930   63
Blavatsky, H(elen) P.
    NIGHTMARE TALES   Theosophical Pub Soc   1892   133   Ill.
Bleiler, Everett and Dikty, T. E. (Editors)
    FRONTIERS IN SPACE   Bantam   1955   166
      Book: selections from BEST SCIENCE FICTION STORIES 1951 - 1952 - 1953
    IMAGINATION UNLIMITED   Berkley   1959   172
      Book: same Abr.
Blish, James
    A CASE OF CONSCIENCE   Ballantine   1958   188
    EARTHMAN, COME HOME   Avon   1956   191
      Book: same Abr.
    ESPER   Avon   1956   190
      Book: JACK OF EAGLES
    THE FROZEN STAR   Ballantine   1957   155
      Book: FALLEN STAR
    GALACTIC CLUSTER   Signet   1959   176
      Book: same
    JACK OF EAGLES   Galaxy Novel   1953   126
      Book: same   (See ibid, ESPER)

Blish, James (Cont.)
   THE NIGHT SHAPES   Ballantine   1962   125
   THE SEEDLING STARS   Signet   1959   158
      Book: same
   THE STAR DWELLERS   Avon   1963   128
      Book: same
   TITAN'S DAUGHTER   Berkley   1961   142
   THE TRIUMPH OF TIME   Avon   1958   158
      Book: same
   VOR   Avon   1955   159
   THE WARRIORS OF DAY   Galaxy Novel   1953   126
   YEAR 2018   Avon   1957   159
      Book: THEY SHALL HAVE STARS
Blish, James and Lowndes, Robert
   THE DUPLICATED MAN   Airmont   1964   128
      Book: same
Bloch, Robert
   ATOMS AND EVIL   Fawcett   1962   160
   BOGEY MEN   Pyramid   1963   159
   HORROR - 7   Belmont   1963   125
      Book: 7 stories from PLEASANT DREAMS and THE OPENER OF THE WAY
   NIGHTMARES   Belmont   1961   140
      Book: PLEASANT DREAMS Abr.
   MORE NIGHTMARES   Belmont   1962   173
      Book: 10 stories from PLEASANT DREAMS and THE OPENER OF THE WAY
   THE SCARF OF PASSION   Avon   1949   154
      Book: THE SCARF
   SEA KISSED   Utopia Pubn   nd   39
   TALES IN A JUGULAR VEIN   Pyramid   1964   156
Boccaccio, Giovanni
   TALES FROM THE DECAMERON   Pocket Books   1956   370
      Book: same Abr.
Boland, John
   WHITE AUGUST   Digit Books   nd   189
      Book: same
Bond, Nelson S.
   THE ADVENTURES OF LANCELOT BIGGS   Consol   London   nd   186
      Book: LANCELOT BIGGS: SPACEMAN
   EXILES OF TIME   Paperback Library   1965   166
      Book: same
   NO TIME LIKE THE FUTURE   Avon   1954   221
Bone, J. F.
   THE LANI PEOPLE   Bantam   1962   152
Boothby, Guy
   THE KIDNAPPED PRESIDENT   Westbrook   Cleveland   1902   191
Boucher, Anthony
   FAR AND AWAY   Ballantine   1955   168
      Book: same
   ROCKET TO THE MORGUE   Dell   1946   223
Boucher, Anthony and McComas, J. Francis (Editors)
   THE BEST FROM FANTASY AND SCIENCE FICTION: 3rd Series   Ace   1959   256
      Book: same

Boucher, Anthony (Editor)
   THE BEST FROM FANTASY AND SCIENCE FICTION: 4th Series   Ace   1960   250
     Book: same
   THE BEST FROM FANTASY AND SCIENCE FICTION: 5th Series   Ace   1961   253
     Book: same
   THE BEST FROM FANTASY AND SCIENCE FICTION: 6th Series   Ace   1962   259
     Book: same
   THE BEST FROM FANTASY AND SCIENCE FICTION: 7th Series   Ace   1962   252
     Book: same
   THE BEST FROM FANTASY AND SCIENCE FICTION: 8th Series   Ace   1963   224
     Book: same
Boulle, Pierre
   PLANET OF THE APES   Signet   1965   157
Bounds, S. J.
   DIMENSION OF HORROR   Panther   1954   159
     Book: same
Bowen, Elizabeth
   STORIES   Vintage   1960   178
Bowen, John
   AFTER THE RAIN   Ballantine   1959   158
     Book: same
Brack, Vektis
   CASTAWAY FROM SPACE   Gannet   1953   128
   ODYSSEY IN SPACE   Gannet   nd   127
   THE "X" PEOPLE   Gannet   1953   128
Brackett, Leigh
   THE LONG TOMORROW   Ace   1962   223
     Book: same
   SECRET OF SINHARET   Ace   1964   95
     with PEOPLE OF THE TALISMAN   Ace   1964   128
   SHADOW OVER MARS   Pemberton   Manchester   1951   128
   ALPHA CENTAURI OR DIE   Ace   1963   121
     with Wallis LEGEND OF LOST EARTH
   THE BIG JUMP   Ace   1955   131
     with Dick SOLAR LOTTERY
   THE GALACTIC BREED   Ace   1955   151   Book: THE STARMEN
     with Williams CONQUEST OF THE SPACE SEA
   THE NEMESIS FROM TERRA   Ace   1961   120
     with Silverberg COLLISION COURSE
   SWORD OF RHIANNON   Ace   1953   133
     with Howard CONAN THE CONQUEROR
Bradbury, Ray
   FAHRENHEIT 451   Ballantine   1953   202
     Book: same
   THE GOLDEN APPLES OF THE SUN   Bantam   1954   169
     Book: same
   THE ILLUSTRATED MAN   Bantam   1952   186
     Book: same
   THE MARTIAN CHRONICLES   Bantam   1951   181
     Book: same
   A MEDICINE FOR MELANCHOLY   Bantam   1960   183
     Book: same
   THE OCTOBER COUNTRY   Ballantine   1956   276
     Book: same - mostly a reprint of DARK CARNIVAL

Briney, Robert E. (Editor)
   SHANADU   S. S. R.   North Tonawanda, N. Y.   1953   101
Bromfield, Louis
   THE STRANGE CASE OF MISS ANNIE SPRAGGE   Berkley   1956   219
      Book: same
Brooks, Byron A.
   EARTH REVISITED   Arena Pub Co   Boston   1893   137
Brown, Charles Brockden
   WIELAND, OR, THE TRANSFORMATION   Dolphin   1962   276
      Book: same
Brown, Charles Edward
   GHOST TALES; SHORT STORIES FOR USE AT THE FIRESIDE AND CAMP FIRE   Pub by
      the Author   Madison, Wisc.   1931   25
Brown, Fredric
   HONEYMOON IN HELL   Bantam   1958   150
   THE LIGHTS IN THE SKY ARE STARS   Bantam   1955   149
      Book: same
   MARTIANS, GO HOME   Bantam   1956   159
      Book: same
   THE MIND THING   Bantam   1961   149
   NIGHTMARES AND GEEZENSTACKS   Bantam   1961   137
   ROGUE IN SPACE   Bantam   1957   163
      Book: same
   SPACE ON MY HANDS   Bantam   1953   239
      Book: same
   STAR SHINE   Bantam   1956   138
      Book: ANGELS AND SPACESHIPS
   WHAT MAD UNIVERSE?   Bantam   1950   183
      Book: same
Brown, Fredric and Reynolds, Mack (Editors)
   SCIENCE FICTION CARNIVAL   Bantam   1957   167
      Book: same
Brown, George Sheldon
   DESTINATION MARS   Self   nd   128
   THE PLANETOID PERIL   Self   1952   128
   THE YELLOW PLANET   Self   1954   100
Brown, Rosel G.
   A HANDFUL OF TIME   Ballantine   1962   160
Brunner, John
   CASTAWAY'S WORLD   Ace   1963   127
      with THE RITES OF ONE   Ace   1963   129
   THE DREAMING EARTH   Pyramid   1963   159
   THE SPACE-TIME JUGGLER   Ace   1963   84
      with THE ASTRONAUTS MUST NOT LAND   Ace   1963   138
   THE SUPER BARBARIANS   Ace   1962   160
   TO CONQUER CHAOS   Ace   1964   192
   THE WHOLE MAN   Ballantine   1964   188
   THE ALTAR OF ASCONEL   Ace   1965   122
      with White ANDROID AVENGER
   THE ATLANTIC ABOMINATION   Ace   1961   128
      with Grinnell THE MARTIAN MISSILE
   ECHO IN THE SKULL   Ace   1960   94
      with Nourse ROCKET TO LIMBO

Bulmer, Kenneth
  BEYOND THE SILVER SKY   Ace   1961   100
    with Brunner MEETING AT INFINITY
  THE CHANGELING WORLDS   Ace   1959   145
    with Anderson VANGUARD FROM ALPHA
  CITY UNDER THE SEA   Ace   1958   175
    with Anderson STAR WAYS
  DEMON'S WORLD   Ace   1964   139
    with Purdom I WANT THE STARS
  THE EARTH GODS ARE COMING   Ace   1960   107
    with St. Clair THE GAMES OF NEITH
  LAND BEYOND THE MAP   Ace   1965   136
    with Hamilton FUGITIVE OF THE STARS
  THE MILLION YEAR HUNT   Ace   1964   133
    with Leibor SHIPS TO THE STARS
  NO MAN'S WORLD   Ace   1961   128
    with Anderson MAYDAY ORBIT
  THE SECRET OF ZI   Ace   1959   161
    with Cummings BEYOND THE VANISHING POINT
  WIZARD OF STARSHIP POSEIDON   Ace   1963   124
    with Anderson LET THE SPACEMEN BEWARE
Burke, Jonathan
  THE DARK GATEWAY   Hamilton   1953   223
  THE ECHOING WORLDS   Panther   1954   159
    Book: same
  TWILIGHT OF REASON   Hamilton   1954   159
Burke, Thomas
  LIMEHOUSE NIGHTS   Digit Books   1961   156
    Book: same
Burks, Arthur J.
  THE GREAT MIRROR   Swan   1952   128
  LOOK BEHIND YOU   Shroud Pub   Buffalo, N. Y.   1954   73
Burnett, Whit and Hallie (Editors)
  19 TALES OF TERROR   Bantam   1957   229
  THINGS WITH CLAWS   Ballantine   1961   159
Burroughs, Edgar Rice
  APACHE DEVIL   Ballantine   1964   192
    Book: same
  AT THE EARTH'S CORE   Ace   1962   142
    Book: same
  BACK TO THE STONE AGE   Ace   1964   221
    Book: same
  THE BEASTS OF TARZAN   Ace   1963   191
    Book: same
  BEYOND THE FARTHEST STAR   Ace   1964   125
    Book: TALES OF THREE PLANETS first part
  CARSON OF VENUS   Ace   1964   192
    Book: same
  THE CAVE GIRL   Ace   1964   224
    Book: same
  THE CHESSMEN OF MARS   Ace   1962   224
    Book: same
  ESCAPE ON VENUS   Ace   1964   254
    Book: same

Burroughs, Edgar Rice (Cont.)
THE ETERNAL SAVAGE   Ace   1964   192
    Book: THE ETERNAL LOVER
A FIGHTING MAN OF MARS   Ace   1963   253
    Book: same
THE GODS OF MARS   Ballantine   1963   190
    Book: same
JOHN CARTER OF MARS   Ballantine   1965   157
    Book: same
JUNGLE TALES OF TARZAN   Ace   1963   220
    Book: same
THE LAD AND THE LION   Ballantine   1964   192
    Book: same
THE LAND OF HIDDEN MEN   Ace   1964   191
    Book: JUNGLE GIRL
LAND OF TERROR   Ace   1964   175
    Book: same
THE LAND THAT TIME FORGOT   Ace   1963   125
    Book: LAND THAT TIME FORGOT first part
LLANA OF GATHOL   Ballantine   1963   191
    Book: same
THE LOST CONTINENT   Ace   1964   123
    Book: BEYOND THIRTY and THE MAN-EATER first part
LOST ON VENUS   Ace   1964   192
    Book: same
THE MAD KING   Ace   1964   255
    Boo : same
THE MASTERMIND OF MARS   Ace   1962   159
    Book: THE MASTER MIND OF MARS
THE MONSTER MEN   Ace   1962   159
    Book: same
THE MOON MAID   Ace   1962   176
    Book: THE MOON MAID first part
THE MOON MEN   Ace   1962 · 222
    Book: THE MOON MAID second part
OUT OF TIME'S ABYSS   Ace   1964   125
    Book: LAND THAT TIME FORGOT third part
PELLUCIDAR   Ace   1962   160
    Book: same
THE PEOPLE THAT TIME FORGOT   Ace   1964   124
    Book: LAND THAT TIME FORGOT second part
THE PIRATES OF VENUS   Ace   1962   173
    Book: same
A PRINCESS OF MARS   Ballantine   1963   159
    Book: same
THE RETURN OF TARZAN   Ballantine   1963   221
    Book: same
SAVAGE PELLUCIDAR   Ace   1964   221
    Book: same
THE SON OF TARZAN   Ace   1963   255
    Book: same
SWORDS OF MARS   Ballantine   1963   191
    Book: same

Burroughs, Edgar Rice (Cont.)
    SYNTHETIC MEN OF MARS   Ballantine   1963   160
      Book: same
    TANAR OF PELLUCIDAR   Ace   1962   224
      Book: same
    TARZAN AND THE ANT MEN   Ballantine   1963   188
      Book: same
    TARZAN AND THE CITY OF GOLD   Ace   1963   191
      Book: same
    TARZAN AND THE FORBIDDEN CITY   Ballantine   1964   191
      Book: same
    TARZAN AND THE FOREIGN LEGION   Ballantine   1964   192
      Book: same
    TARZAN AND THE GOLDEN LION   Ballantine   1963   191
      Book: same
    TARZAN AND THE JEWELS OF OPAR   Ace   1963   192
      Book: same
    TARZAN AND THE LEOPARD MEN   Ballantine   1964   192
      Book: same
    TARZAN AND THE LION MAN   Ace   1963   223
      Book: same
    TARZAN AND THE LOST EMPIRE   Ace   1963   192
      Book: same
    TARZAN AND THE MADMAN   Ballantine   1965   160
      Book: same
    TARZAN AT THE EARTH'S CORE   Ace   1963   223
      Book: same
    TARZAN, LORD OF THE JUNGLE   Pinnacle   London   1958   192
      Book: same
    TARZAN OF THE APES   Ballantine   1963   219
      Book: same
    TARZAN THE INVINCIBLE   Ace   1963   220
      Book: same
    TARZAN THE MAGNIFICENT   Ballantine   1964   192
      Book: same
    TARZAN THE TERRIBLE   Ballantine   1963   220
      Book: same
    TARZAN THE UNTAMED   Ballantine   1963   254
      Book: same
    TARZAN TRIUMPHANT   Ace   1963   222
      Book: same
    TARZAN'S QUEST   Ballantine   1964   192
      Book: same
    THUVIA, MAID OF MARS   Ace   1963   143
      Book: same
    THE WAR CHIEF   Ballantine   1964   190
      Book: same
    THE WARLORD OF MARS   Ballantine   1963   220
      Book: same
Burton, Edmund
    IN QUEST OF THE GOLDEN ORCHID   Cole   Worthing, England   nd   80
    PERIL OF CREATION   U. T. B.   London   nd   33
    THE RADIUM KING   Cole   Worthing, England   nd   86

Burton, Richard (Translator)
    TALES FROM THE ARABIAN NIGHTS   Pocket Books   1954   411
        Book: same Abr.
Butler, Joan
    DEEP FREEZE   Hamilton   1953   128
        Book: same
Butler, Samuel
    EREWHON   Signet   1961   240
        Book: same

Cabell, James Branch
    JURGEN   Xanadu (Crown)   nd   368
        Book: same
Caldwell, Taylor
    YOUR SINS AND MINE   Fawcett   1955   127
Cameron, Berl
    BLACK INFINITY   Warren   1952   127
    COSMIC ECHELON   Warren   1952   128
    DESTINATION ALPHA   Warren   1952   127
    LOST AEONS   Warren   1953   159
    PHOTOMESIS   Warren   1952   127
    SPHERO NOVA   Warren   1952   159
    SOLAR GRAVITA   Warren   1953   159
Campbell, H. J.
    ANOTHER SPACE - ANOTHER TIME   Panther   1954   159
        Book: same
    BRAIN ULTIMATE   Hamilton   1953   157
        Book: same
    CHAOS IN MINIATURE   Hamilton   nd   109
    THE LAST MUTATION   Hamilton   nd   109
    MICE OR MACHINES   Hamilton   nd   109
    THE MOON IS HEAVEN   Hamilton   nd   110
    ONCE UPON A SPACE   Hamilton   1954   142
    THE RED PLANET   Panther   1954   159
        Book: same
    WORLD IN A TEST TUBE   Hamilton   nd   106
Campbell, H. J. (Editor)
    TOMORROW'S UNIVERSE   Hamilton   1953   224
Campbell, John W., Jr.
    BRIGANDS OF THE MOON   Dutchess Printing   Toronto   1951   191
    THE THING AND OTHER STORIES   Kemsley Newspapers   London   1952   190
        Book: WHO GOES THERE?
    THE MOON IS HELL   Fantasy Press   Reading, Pa.   1951   256
        Book: same
    WHO GOES THERE?   Dell   1955   254
        Book: same
Campbell, John W., Jr. (Editor)
    ASTOUNDING SCIENCE FICTION ANTHOLOGY   Berkley   1956   192
        Book: ASTOUNDING SCIENCE FICTION ANTHOLOGY   8 stories,from
    ASTOUNDING TALES OF SPACE AND TIME   Berkley   1957   190
        Book: ASTOUNDING SCIENCE FICTION ANTHOLOGY   7 stories from
Cantor, Hal (Editor)
    GHOSTS AND THINGS   Berkley   1962   160

Capek, Karel
    WAR WITH THE NEWTS   Bantam   1955   236
        Book: same
Capote, Truman
    THE GRASS HARP and A TREE OF NIGHT   Signet   1956   216
        Book: same
    OTHER VOICES, OTHER ROOMS   Signet   1949   127
        Book: same
Carnell, E. J.
    THE MALE RESPONSE   Beacon (Galaxy Novel)   1961   159
Carnell, John (Editor)
    THE BEST FROM NEW WORLDS   Boardman   London   1955   156
    LAMBDA I AND OTHERS   Berkley   1964   175
Carnell, Ted (Editor)
    JINN AND JITTERS   Pendulum   London   1946   116
Carr, John Dickson
    THE BURNING COURT   Bantam   1954   215
        Book: same
    CASTLE SKULL   Berkley   1960   142
        Book: same
    THE DEVIL IN VELVET   Bantam   1952   312
        Book: same
Carr, Robert Spencer
    BEYOND INFINITY   Dell   1952   223
        Book: same
Carr, Terry
    WARLORD OF KOR   Ace   1963   97
        with Williams THE STAR WASPS
Carroll, Leslie
    YOU CAN'T HANG THE DEAD   Mitre Press   nd   31
Carroll, Lewis
    ALICE IN WONDERLAND   Signet   1960   238
        Book: same
Carter, Dee
    BLUE CORDON   Warren   1952   128
        Book: same
    CHLOROPLASM   Warren   1952   159
    PURPLE ISLANDS   Warren   1953   159
        Book: same
Carter, Nick
    FIGHTING AGAINST MILLIONS   Street & Smith   1893   229
Carter, Lin
    THE WIZARD OF LEMURIA   Ace   1965   127
Cartmill, V. H. and Grayson, Charles
    THE GOLDEN ARGOSY   Bantam   1956   405
        Book: same
Castle, Jeffery Lloyd
    SATELLITE E ONE   Bantam   1958   164
        Book: same
Cave, Hugh B.
    THE CROSS ON THE DRUM   Ace   1959   287
        Book: same
Cerf, Bennett, (Editor)
    STORIES SELECTED FROM THE UNEXPECTED   Bantam   1963   184
        Book: THE UNEXPECTED Abr.

Christopher, John (Cont.)
   PLANET IN PERIL   Avon   1958   159
   THE TWENTY-SECOND CENTURY   Lancer   1962   190
     Book: same
   WHITE VOYAGE   Avon   1965   190
Clarke, Arthur
   AGAINST THE FALL OF NIGHT   Pyramid   1960   159
     Book: same
   CHILDHOOD'S END   Ballantine   1953   214
     Book: same
   THE CITY AND THE STARS   Signet   1957   191
     Book: same   (completely re-written version of AGAINST THE FALL OF NIGHT
   THE DEEP RANGE   Signet   1958   175
     Book: same
   EARTHLIGHT   Ballantine   1955   155
     Book: same
   EXPEDITION TO EARTH   Ballantine   1953   165
     Book: same
   A FALL OF MOONDUST   Dell   1963   240
     Book: same
   ISLANDS IN THE SKY   Signet   1960   127
     Book: same
   MASTER OF SPACE   Lancer   1962   158
     PRELUDE TO SPACE
   THE OTHER SIDE OF THE SKY   Signet   1959   160
     Book: same
   PRELUDE TO SPACE   Ballantine   1954   166
     Book: same
   REACH FOR TOMORROW   Ballantine   1956   166
     Book: same
   SANDS OF MARS   Pocket Books   1954   217
     Book: same
   TALES FROM THE WHITE HART   Ballantine   1957   161
   TALES OF TEN WORLDS   Dell   1964   188
     Book: same
Clarke, A. V. and Bulmer, H. K.
   CYBERNETIC CONTROLLER   Hamilton   1952   112
   SPACE TREASON   Hamilton   1952   112
Clement, Hal
   CLOSE TO CRITICAL   Ballantine   1964   190
   CYCLE OF FIRE   Ballantine   1957   185
   FROM OUTER SPACE   Avon   1957   188
     Book: NEEDLE
   MISSION OF GRAVITY   Pyramid   1962   174
     Book: same
   NATIVES OF SPACE   Ballantine   1965   156
Clifton, Mark
   EIGHT KEYS TO EDEN   Ballantine   1962   160
     Book: same
   WHEN THEY COME FROM SPACE   Macfadden-Bartell   1963   144
     Book: same
Clifton, Mark and Riley, Frank
   THE FOREVER MACHINE   Galaxy Novel   1958   159
     Book: THEY'D RATHER BE RIGHT

Clingerman, Mildred
  A CUPFUL OF SPACE   Ballantine   1961   142
Coates, Robert M.
  THE EATER OF DARKNESS   Capricorn (Putnam)   1959   238
    Book: same
Cobb, Weldon J.
  A TRIP TO MARS   Street & Smith   1901   320
Coblentz, Stanton A.
  HIDDEN WORLD   Airmont   1964   127
    Book: same
  INTO PLUTONIAN DEPTHS   Avon   1950   159
  THE PLANET OF YOUTH   Fantasy Pub Co   Los Angeles   1952   71
  THE SUNKEN WORLD   Kemsley Newspapers   London   1951   190
    Book: same
  YOUTH MADNESS   Utopia Pubn   nd   36
Cockcroft, W. P.
  THEY CAME FROM MARS   Swan   nd   16
Cody, C. S.
  THE WITCHING NIGHT   Dell   1954   256
    Book: same
Cogswell, Theodore R.
  THE WALL AROUND THE WORLD   Pyramid   1962   160
Collier, John
  DEFY THE FOUL FIEND   Penguin   1948   295
    Book: same
  FANCIES AND GOODNIGHTS   Bantam   1953   375
    Book: same
  GREEN THOUGHTS AND OTHER STRANGE TALES   Armed Forces Edition   nd   287
    Book: GREEN THOUGHTS and selection from other books
Collins, Charles M. (Editor)
  FRIGHT   Avon   1963   141
Collins, Hunt
  TOMORROW AND TOMORROW   Pyramid   1956   190
    Book: TOMORROW'S WORLD
Collins, Mabel
  SUGGESTION   Lovell   nd   276
    Book: same
Collins, Wilkie
  THE DREAM-WOMAN   Happy Hours Library   nd   95
    with Doyle, A. Conan MY FRIEND THE MURDERER
Collins, Wilkie and Others
  THE HAUNTED HOTEL AND 25 OTHER GHOST STORIES   Avon   1941   255
Condray, Bruno G.
  THE DISSENTIZENS   Tit-Bits S-F Library   London   nd   64
Congdon, Michael and Don (Editors)
  ALONE BY NIGHT   Ballantine   1961   144
Congdon, Don (Editor)
  TALES OF LOVE AND HORROR   Ballantine   1961   144
Conklin, Groff (Editor)
  THE BIG BOOK OF SCIENCE FICTION   Berkley   1957   187
    Book: same Abr.
  BR-R-R!   Avon   1959   192
  CROSSROADS IN TIME   Permabooks   1953   312
  DIMENSION 4   Pyramid   1964   159

Conklin, Groff (Editor) (Cont.)
   FIVE ODD   Pyramid   1964   188
   FOUR FOR THE FUTURE   Pyramid   1959   160
   THE GRAVEYARD READER   Ballantine   1958   188
   GREAT SCIENCE FICTION BY SCIENTISTS   Collier   1962   313
   IN THE GRIP OF TERROR   Permabooks   1951   364
   INVADERS OF EARTH   Tempo (Grosset)   1962   382
     Book: same
   OPERATION FUTURE   Permabooks   1955   356
   POSSIBLE WORLDS OF SCIENCE FICTION   Berkley   1958   188
     Book: same
   SCIENCE FICTION ADVENTURES IN DIMENSION   Berkley   1965   168
     Book: same Abr.
   SCIENCE FICTION ADVENTURES IN MUTATION   Berkely   1965   170
     Book: same Abr.
   THE SCIENCE FICTION GALAXY   Permabooks   1950   242
   SCIENCE FICTION OMNIBUS   Berkley   1956   190
     Book: OMNIBUS OF SCIENCE FICTION
   SCIENCE FICTION TERROR TALES   Pocket Books   1955   262
     Book: same   Abr.
   SCIENCE FICTION THINKING MACHINES   Bantam   1955   183
     Book: same Abr.
   SIX GREAT SHORT NOVELS OF SCIENCE FICTION   Dell   1954   384
   17 X INFINITY   Dell   1963   272
   THE SUPERNATURAL READER   Collier   1962   352
     Book: same
   13 GREAT STORIES OF SCIENCE FICTION   Fawcett   1960   192
   A TREASURY OF SCIENCE FICTION   Berkely   1956   186
     Book: same Abr.
   WORLDS OF WHEN   Pyramid   1962   159
Conquest, Robert
   A WORLD OF DIFFERENCE   Ballantine   1964   192
Conroy, Rick
   MARTIANS IN A FROZEN WORLD   Hamilton   nd   108
   MISSION FROM MARS   Hamilton   1952   112
Cook, William Wallace
   ADRIFT IN THE UNKNOWN   Street & Smith   1905   305
   CAST AWAY AT THE POLE   Street & Smith   1904   311
   THE EIGHTH WONDER   Street & Smith   1907   318
   MAROONED IN 1492   Street & Smith   1905   307
   A ROUND TRIP TO THE YEAR 2000   Street & Smith   1903   310
Coombs, Charles
   THE MYSTERY OF SATELLITE 7   Tempo (Grosset)   1962   192
     Book: same
Coon, Horace
   43,000 YEARS LATER   Signet   1958   143
Cooper, Edmund
   DEADLY IMAGE   Ballantine   1958   190
   SEED OF LIGHT   Ballantine   1959   159
   TOMORROW'S GIFT   Ballantine   1958   164
   TRANSIT   Lancer   1964   159
     Book: same
Coppard, A. E.
   ADAM AND EVE AND PINCH ME   Penguin   1946   168
     Book: same

Coppel, Alfred
   DARK DECEMBER   Fawcett   1960   208
Correy, Lee
   CONTRABAND ROCKET   Ace   1956   175
        with Leinster THE FORGOTTEN PLANET
Cozzens, James Gould
   CASTAWAY   Bantam   1952   121
        Book: same
Crane, Robert
   HERO'S WALK   Ballantine   1954   196
        Book: same
Crispin, Edmund (Editor)
   BEST S F: SCIENCE FICTION STORIES   Faber & Faber   London   1958   368
        Book: same
   BEST S F TWO   Faber & Faber   London   1959   357
        Book: same
Cross, John Keir
   STORIES FROM THE OTHER PASSENGER   Ballantine   1961   159
        Book: THE OTHER PASSENGER Abr.
Crossen, Kendall Foster
   YEAR OF CONSENT   Dell   1954   224
Cummings, Ray
   BEYOND THE STARS   Ace   1963   160
   A BRAND NEW WORLD   Ace   1964   158
   BRIGANDS OF THE MOON   Ace   1959   224
        Book: same
   THE EXILE OF TIME   Ace   1965   176
   INTO THE FOURTH DIMENSION   Swan   nd   128
   THE MAN ON THE METEOR   Swan   1952   128
   THE PRINCESS OF THE ATOM   Avon   1950   158
        Book: same
   THE SHADOW GIRL   Ace   1962   159
        Book: same
   BEYOND THE VANISHING POINT   Ace   1959   95
        with Bulmer THE SECRET OF ZI
   THE MAN WHO MASTERED TIME   Ace   1956   172
        Book: same   with Kelleam OVERLORDS FROM SPACE
   WANDL, THE INVADER   Ace   1961   135
        with Woodcott I SPEAK FOR EARTH

de Vinci, Leonardo
   THE DELUGE   Lion Books   1955   124
        Book: same
Dahl, Roald
   KISS, KISS   Dell   1962   288
        Book: same
   SOMEONE LIKE YOU   Dell   1961   320
        Book: same
Daly, Carroll John
   THE LEGION OF THE LIVING DEAD   Popular Pub   London and Toronto   1947   96
Dane, Donald
   THE ROBOT JU-JU   Champion Library   1936   64
Davenport, Benjamin Rush
   UNCLE SAM'S CABINS   Mascot Pub Co   1895   271

Davenport, Basil (Editor)
    DEALS WITH THE DEVIL   Ballantine   1959   160
      Book: same Abr.
    INVISIBLE MEN   Ballantine   1960   158
    TALES TO BE TOLD IN THE DARK   Ballantine   1957   159
      Book: same Abr.
Davenport, Gentry
    A FRANKISH PAIR   Belford   1890   208
Davidson, Avram
    MASTERS OF THE MAZE   Pyramid   1965   168
    MUTINY IN SPACE   Pyramid   1964   159
    OR ALL THE SEAS WITH OYSTERS   Berkley   1962   176
    WHAT STRANGE STARS AND SKIES   Ace   1965   188
Davies, Valentine
    IT HAPPENS EVERY SPRING   Avon   1950   126
      Book: same
Day, Lionel
    THE BURIED WORLD   Boys' Friend Library   1938   62
de Balzac, Honore
    THE MYSTERIES OF HONORE DE BALZAC   Juniper Press   nd   382
de Camp, L. Sprague
    DIVIDE AND RULE   Lancer   1964   164
      Book: same
    THE HAND OF ZEI   Ace   1962   113
      with THE SEARCH FOR ZEI   Ace   1962   143
        Book: THE SEARCH FOR ZEI
    LEST DARKNESS FALL   Pyramid   1963   174
      Book: same
    ROGUE QUEEN   Dell   1952   192
      Book: same
    THE TOWER OF ZANID   Airmont   1963   127
      Book: same
de Camp, L. Sprague (Editor)
    THE SPELL OF SEVEN   Pyramid   1965   158
    SPRAGUE DE CAMP'S NEW ANTHOLOGY OF SCIENCE FICTION   Hamilton   1953   159
      Book: same
    SWORDS AND SORCERY   Pyramid   1963   186
de Camp, L. Sprague and Miller, P. Schuyler
    GENUS HOMO   Berkley   1961   157
      Book: same
de Camp, L. Sprague and Pratt, Fletcher
    CASTLE OF IRON   Pyramid   1962   159
      Book: same
    THE INCOMPLETE ENCHANTER   Pyramid   1962   192
      Book: same
de Camp, L. Sprague
    COSMIC MANHUNT   Ace   1954   120
      with Simak RING AROUND THE SUN
de la Mars, Walter
    THE RETURN   Pan Books   1955   116
      Book: same
Dee, Roger
    AN EARTH GONE MAD   Ace   1954   144
      with Asimov THE REBELLIOUS STARS

Deegan, Jon J.
   AMATEURS IN ALCHEMY Hamilton 1952 128
   ANTRO, THE LIFE-GIVER Hamilton 1953 144
     Book: same
   BEYOND THE FOURTH DOOR Hamilton 1954 159
   CORRIDORS OF TIME Panther 1954 159
     Book: same
   EXILES IN TIME Hamilton 1954 159
   THE GREAT ONES Panther 1954 159
     Book: same
   UNDERWORLD OF ZELLO Hamilton 1952 128
Defor, Daniel
   TALES OF PIRACY, CRIME AND GHOSTS Penguin 1945 247
del Martia, Astron
   DAWN OF DARKNESS Gaywood Press London 1951 98
   INTERSTELLAR ESPIONAGE Gaywood Press London 1952 100
   SPACE PIRATES Gaywood Press London nd 112
   THE TREMBLING WORLD Gaywood Press London nd 128
del Rey, Lester
   AND SOME WERE HUMAN Ballantine 1959 160
     Book: same
   DAY OF THE GIANTS Airmont 1964 128
     Book: same
   MORTALS AND MONSTERS Ballantine 1965 188
   NERVES Ballantine 1956 153
     Book: same
   ROBOTS AND CHANGELINGS Ballantine 1957 175
Delany, Samuel R.
   THE BALLAD OF BETA - 2 Ace 1965 96
     with Petaja ALPHA YES, TERRA NO!
   CAPTIVES OF THE FLAME Ace 1963 147
     with Woodcott THE PSIONIC MENACE
   CITY OF A THOUSAND SUNS Ace 1965 156
   THE JEWELS OF APTOR Ace 1962 156
     with White SECOND ENDING
   THE TOWERS OF TORON Ace 1964 140
     with Williams THE LUNAR EYE
Derleth, August W.
   MR. GEORGE AND OTHER ODD PERSONS Belmont 1964 176
     Book: same - under pseudonym of Stephan Grendon
   NOT LONG FOR THIS WORLD Ballantine 1959 159
     Book: same Abr.
Derleth, August (Editor)
   BEACHEADS IN SPACE Berkley 1957 190
     Book: same Abr.
   BEYOND TIME AND SPACE Berkley 1954 174
     Book: same Abr.
   THE OTHER SIDE OF THE MOON Berkley 1959 172
     Book: same Abr.
   THE OUTER REACHES Berkley 1958 174
     Book: same Abr.
   STRANGE PORTS OF CALL Berkley 1958 173
     Book: same Abr.

Derleth, August (Editor) (Cont.)
    TIME TO COME   Berkley   1958   189
        Book: same Abr.
    WORLDS OF TOMORROW   Berkley   1958   172
        Book: same Abr.
DeVet, Charles and MacLean, Katherine
    COSMIC CHECKMATE   Ace   1962   96
        with Williams KING OF THE FOURTH PLANET
Di Bibiena, Jean-Galli
    AMOROUS PHILANDRE   Avon   1948   122
Dick, Philip K.
    CLANS OF THE ALPHANE MOON   Ace   1964   192
    DR. BLOODMONEY, OR HOW WE GOT ALONG AFTER THE BOMB   Ace   1965   222
    EYE IN THE SKY   Ace   1957   255
    THE GAME PLAYERS OF TITAN   Ace   1963   191
    MARTIAN TIME SLIP   Ballantine   1964   220
    THE PENULTIMATE TRUTH   Belmont   1964   174
    THE SIMULCRA   Ace   1964   192
    THE VARIABLE MAN   Ace   1958   255
    THE COSMIC PUPPETS   Ace   1957   127
        with North SARGASSO OF SPACE
    DR. FUTURITY   Ace   1960   138
        with Brunner SLAVERS OF SPACE
    THE MAN WHO JAPED   Ace   1956   180
        with Tubb THE SPACE BORN
    SOLAR LOTTERY   Ace   1955   188
        with Brackett THE BIG JUMP
    VULCAN'S HAMMER   Ace   1961   139
        with Brunner THE SKYNAPPERS
    THE WORLD JONES MADE   Ace   1956   192
        with St. Clair AGENT OF THE UNKNOWN
Dickens, Charles
    A CHRISTMAS CAROL   Pocket Books   1958   221
        Book: same
Dickson, Gordon R.
    DELUSION WORLD   Ace   1961   100
        with SPACIAL DELIVERY   Ace   1961   123
    THE GENETIC GENERAL   Ace   1960   159
        with TIME TO TELEPORT   Ace   1960   96
    NAKED TO THE STARS   Pyramid   1961   159
    NO ROOM FOR MAN   Macfadden-Bartell   1963   158
        Book: NECROMANCER
    ALIEN FROM ARCTURUS   Ace   1956   150
        with Williams THE ATOM CURTAIN
    MANKIND ON THE RUN   Ace   1956   151
        with Norton THE CROSSROADS OF TIME
Dikty, T. E. (Editor)
    5 TALES FROM TOMORROW   Fawcett   1957   176
        Book: BEST SCIENCE FICTION STORIES AND NOVELS 1955 Abr.
    6 FROM WORLDS BEYOND   Fawcett   1958   160
        Book: BEST SCIENCE FICTION STORIES AND NOVELS 1956 Abr.
Dinesen, Isak
    WINTER'S TALES   Dell   1957   287
        Book: same

A Diplomat
    THE RISE AND FALL OF THE UNITED STATES. A THIN LEAF FROM HISTORY, A. D. 2060
        Neely   1898   205
Dodd, Anna Bowman
    THE REPUBLIC OF THE FUTURE   Cassell   London and New York   1887   86
Doyle, A. Conan
    THE LOST WORLD   Pyramid   1960   192
        Book: same
    MY FRIEND THE MURDERER   Happy Hours Library   nd   pages 67 to 95
        with Collins THE DREAM-WOMAN
Drury, Allen
    ADVISE AND CONSENT   Pocket Books   1961   760
        Book: same
Duane, Toby and Leverentz, A.
    BLAGUE   S. S. R.   N. Tonawanda, N. Y.   1952   99
DuBois, Theodora
    SOLUTION T-25   Kemsley Newspapers   London   1952   190
        Book: same
Duerrenmatt, Friedrich
    TRAPS   Knopf   1960   115
Duke, Winifred
    DEATH AND HIS SWEETHEART   Jarrolds   London   nd   176
Duncan, David
    BEYOND EDEN   Ballantine   1955   159
        Book: same
    DARK DOMINION   Ballantine   1954   206
        Book: same
    OCCAM'S RAZOR   Ballantine   1957   165
Dundee, Douglas
    CAVE-BOY EREK   Champion Library   1935   63
Dunn, J. Allen
    THE ISLAND OF THE DEAD   Boys' Friend Library   1930   64
Duranty, Walter
    BABIES WITHOUT TAILS   Modern Age   1937   168
Duthie, Eric (Editor)
    TALL SHORT STORIES   Ace   1960   352
        Book: same
Dutourd, Jean
    A DOG'S HEAD   Avon   1963   127
        Book: same
Eddison, E. R.
    THE WORM OUROBOROS   Xanadu (Crown)   nd   348
        Book: same
Edgar, Alfred
    THE INSECT MEN   Boys' Friend Library   1936   87
    INVADERS FROM MARS   Boys' Friend Library   1931   63
Edmondson, G. C.
    THE SHIP THAT SAILED THE TIME STREAM   Ace   1965   167
        with STRANGER THAN YOU THINK   Ace   1965   87
"Edward" (Pseud.)
    THE LABORATORY MEDIUM   Biddle   London   nd   12
Edwards, Norman
    INVASION FROM 2500   Monarch   1964   126

Ehrlich, Max
   THE BIG EYE   Popular Library   1950   223
     Book: same
Einstein, Charles
   THE DAY NEW YORK WENT DRY   Fawcett   1964   160
Elliott, George
   THE CASE OF THE MISSING AIRMAN   Swan   nd   36
Elliot, Lee
   BIO-MUTON   Warren   1952   128
   OVERLORD NEW YORK   Warren   1953   159
     Book: same
   THE THIRD MUTANT   Warren   1953   160
Ellison, Harlan
   ELLISON WONDERLAND   Paperback Library   1962   191
   THE MAN WITH NINE LIVES   Ace   1960   131
     with A TOUCH OF INFINITY   Ace   1960   123
Elwood, Roger (Editor)
   ALIEN WORLDS   Paperback Library   1964   176
   INVASION OF THE ROBOTS   Paperback Library   1965   160
Ely, David
   SECONDS   Signet   1964   159
Endore, Guy
   THE WEREWOLF OF PARIS   Ace   1962   223
     Book: same
Erskine, John
   THE PRIVATE LIFE OF HELEN OF TROY   Popular Library   1948   222
     Book: same
Evans, E. Everett
   MAN OF MANY MINDS   Pyramid   1959   192
     Book: same
Evarts, R. C.
   ALICE'S ADVENTURES IN CAMBRIDGE   Harvard Lampoon   Cambridge, Mass.
     1913   67   ill.
Fairman, Paul W.
   CITY UNDER THE SEA   Pyramid   1965   156
   THE WORLD GRABBERS   Monarch   1964   126
Fane, Bron
   THE GHOUL AND THE GODDESS   Badger   nd   158
   THE INTRUDERS   Badger   nd   158
   JUGGERNAUT   Badger   nd   158
   THE MACABRE ONES   Badger   nd   158
   NEMESIS   Badger   nd   158
   RODENT MUTATION   Badger   nd   158
   SOFTLY BY MOONLIGHT   Badger   nd   158
   SOMEWHERE OUT THERE   Badger   nd   158
   STORM GOD'S FURY   Badger   nd   158
   SUSPENSION   Badger   nd   158
   UNKNOWN DESTINY   Badger   nd   158
Fanthorpe, R. L.
   ASTEROID MAN   Badger   nd   158
   BITTER REFLECTION   Badger   nd   158
   CALL OF THE WILD   Badger   1965   158
   CENTURION'S VENGEANCE   Badger   nd   158
   CURSE OF THE TOTEM   Badger   nd   158

Fast, Julius (Editor)
    OUT OF THIS WORLD   Penguin   1944   252
Fawley, Wilbur
    SHUDDERING CASTLE   Dutchess Printing   Toronto   1950   128
        Book: same
Fearn, John Russell
    EMPEROR OF MARS   Hamilton   nd   127
    GODDESS OF MARS   Hamilton   nd   126
    OPERATION VENUS   Scion, Ltd.   nd   128
    RED MEN OF MARS   Hamilton   nd   127
    SLAVES OF IJAX   Koner   Llandudno, Wales   nd   80
    WARRIOR OF MARS   Hamilton   nd   127
Forman, Joseph W. (Editor)
    NO LIMITS   Ballantine   1964   192
Fossier, Michael
    FULLY DRESSED AND IN HIS RIGHT MIND   Lion Books   1954   126
        Book: same
Fidel, I. N. and Hook, A.
    CHRONICLES OF SIMON CHRISTIANUS AND HIS MANIFOLD AND WONDROUS ADVENTURES IN
        THE LAND OF COSMOS   Bennett   nd   110
Field, Gans R.
    ROMANCE IN BLACK: A THRILLING NOVEL   Utopia Pubn   nd   64
Figgis, Darrell
    THE RETURN OF THE HERO   Boni   1930   221
Finn, Ralph L.
    CAPTIVE ON THE FLYING SAUCERS   Gaywood Press   London   nd   123
    FREAKS AGAINST SUPERMEN   Gaywood Press   London   nd   123
Finnery, Charles G.
    THE CIRCUS OF DR. LAO   Compass Books   1961   160
        Book: same
    THE GHOSTS OF MANACLE   Pyramid   1964   159
Finney, Jack
    THE BODY SNATCHERS   Dell   1955   191
        Book: same
    THE THIRD LEVEL   Dell   1959   192
        Book: same
Firth, N. Wesley
    SPAWN OF THE VAMPIRE   Bear   London   nd   80
    TERROR STRIKES   Hamilton   nd   80
Fischer, Leonard
    LET OUT THE BEAST   News Stand Library   Toronto   1950   159
Fisher, Vardis
    DARKNESS AND THE DEEP   Pyramid   1960   256
        Book: same
    THE GOLDEN ROOMS   Pyramid   1960   256
        Book: same
Fitzgibbon, Constantine
    WHEN THE KISSING HAD TO STOP   Bantam   1961   230
        Book: same
Flaubert, Gustavo
    SALAMBO   Berkley   1955   253
        Book: same
Flackes, B.
    DUEL IN NIGHTMARE WORLDS   Hamilton   1952   112

Flagg, Francis
    THE NIGHT PEOPLE   Fantasy Pub   Los Angeles   1947   32
Flammarion, Camille
    URANIA   Donohue   Chicago   nd   245
        Book: same
Flecker, James Elroy
    THE LAST GENERATION   New Age   London   1908   56
Fles, Barthold (Editor)
    THE SATURDAY EVENING POST FANTASY STORIES   Avon   1951   126
Foley, Martha (Editor)
    THE BEST AMERICAN SHORT STORIES: 1955   Ballantine   1956   422
Fontenay, Charles L.
    THE DAY THE OCEANS OVERFLOWED   Monarch   1964   128
    REBELS OF THE RED PLANET   Ace   1961   142
        with McIntosh 200 YEARS TO CHRISTMAS
    TWICE UPON A TIME   Ace   1958   152
        with Tubb THE MECHANICAL MONARCH
Forster, E. M.
    THE ETERNAL MOMENT   Universal Library   1964   245
        Book: same
    A PASSAGE TO INDIA   Penguin   1946   299
        Book: same
Foster, L. B.
    THE HOCUS ROOT   Hogbin, Poole   Sydney   nd   155
Foster, Richard
    THE REST MUST DIE   Fawcett   1959   176
Fox, Gardner
    FIVE WEEKS IN A BALLOON   Pyramid   1962   158
        Book: based on Verne FIVE WEEKS IN A BALLOON
    WARRIOR OF LLARN   Ace   1964   160
    ARSENAL OF MIRACLES   Ace   1964   156
        with Brunner THE ENDLESS SHADOW
Fox, Leslie H.
    THE VAMPIRE AND SIXTEEN OTHER STORIES   Alliance Press   London   nd   32
Frank, Pat
    FORBIDDEN AREA   Bantam   1957   214
        Book: same
France, Anatole
    THE REVOLT OF THE ANGELS   Xanadu (Crown)   nd   348
        Book: same
Frank, Pat
    ALAS, BABYLON   Bantam   1960   279
        Book: same
    MR. ADAM   Pocket Books   1948   204
        Book: same
Franklin, Jay
    RAT RACE   Galaxy Novel   1952   126
        Book: same
Frazee, Steve
    THE SKY BLOCK   Pyramid   1958   192
        Book: same
Friend, Oscar J.
    THE KID FROM MARS   Kemsley Newspapers   London   1951   190
        Book: same

Gernsback, Hugo
    RALPH 124C 41   Fawcett   1958   142
        Book: same
Gibbons, Stella
    COLD COMFORT FARM   Penguin   1938   248
        Book: same
Gillon, Diana and Meir
    THE UNSLEEP   Ballantine   1962   207
        Book: same
Gilson, (Capt.) Charles
    THE LOST CITY   Lutterworth Press   London   1940   224
Glynn, A. A.
    PLAN FOR CONQUEST   Badger   nd   158
Godber, Noel
    KEEP IT DARK   Long   London   nd   160
Godwin, Tom
    THE SPACE BARBARIANS   Pyramid   1964   169
    SPACE PRISON   Pyramid   1960   158
        Book: THE SURVIVORS
Gold, H. L. (Editor)
    BODYGUARD   Pocket Books   1962   273
        Book: same
    FIVE GALAXY SHORT NOVELS   Pocket Books   1960   292
        Book: same
    THE THIRD GALAXY READER   Pocket Books   1960   235
        Book: same
    THE FOURTH GALAXY READER   Pocket Books   1960   239
        Book: same
    THE FIFTH GALAXY READER   Pocket Books   1962   233
        Book: same
    MIND PARTNER   Pocket Books   1963   217
        Book: same
    THE WEIRD ONES   Belmont   1962   173
    THE WORLD THAT COULDN'T BE   Pocket Books   1961   260
        Book: same
Golding, Louis
    THE CALL OF THE HAND   Poynings Press   Wineham, Sussex   1944   32
Golding, William
    LORD OF THE FLIES   Capricorn (Putnam)   1959   192
        Book: same
Golding, William and Wyndham, John and Peake, Mervyn
    SOMETIME NEVER   Ballantine   1957   185
Gordon, Rex
    FIRST ON MARS   Ace   1957   192
        Book: NO MAN FRIDAY
    FIRST THROUGH TIME   Ace   1962   160
    FIRST TO THE STARS   Ace   1959   190
Green, Joseph L.
    THE LOAFERS OF REFUGE   Ballantine   1965   160
Greenberg, Martin (Editor)
    MEN AGAINST THE STARS   Pyramid   1957   191
        Book: same Abr.
Gregory, Dave
    LORD OF THE INCAS   Foys' Friend Library   1935   87

Gregory, Franklin
   THE WHITE WOLF   Novel Selections   nd   128
      Book: same
Grey, Charles
   DYNASTY OF DOOM   Milestone   1953   126
   HAND OF HAVOC   Milestone   1954   116
   ENTERPRISE 2115   Milestone   nd   160
   THE EXTRA MAN   Milestone   1954   128
   FUGITIVE OF TIME   Milestone   1953   128
   I FIGHT FOR MARS   Milestone   1953   128
   SPACE HUNGER   Milestone   1953   128
   TORMENTED CITY   Milestone   1953   126
   THE WALL   Milestone   nd   128
Gridban, Volsted
   ALIEN UNIVERSE   Scion, Ltd   1952   no pagination
   DE BRACY'S DRUG   Scion, Ltd   1953   127
   THE DYNO-DEPRESSANT   Scion, Ltd   1953   128
   EXIT LIFE   Scion, Ltd   1953   128
   THE FROZEN LIMIT   Scion, Ltd   1954   128
   THE GENIAL DINOSAUR   Scion, Ltd   1954   128
   I CAME - I SAW - I CONQUERED   Scion, Ltd   1954   126
   THE LONELY ASTRONOMER   Scion, Ltd   1954   128
   MAGNETIC BRAIN   Scion, Ltd   1953   128
   THE MASTER MUST DIE   Scion, Ltd   1953   128
   MOONS FOR SALE   Scion, Ltd   1953   128
   PLANETARY DISPOSALS, LTD.   Scion, Ltd   1953   112
   THE PURPLE WIZARD   Scion, Ltd   1953   128
   REVERSE UNIVERSE   Scion, Ltd   1952   128
   SCOURGE OF THE ATOM   Scion, Ltd   1953   128
   A THING OF THE PAST   Scion, Ltd   1953   128
Grinnell, David
   ACROSS TIME   Ace   1958   150
      Book: same   with Silverberg INVADERS FROM EARTH
   DESTINY'S ORBIT   Ace   1962   114
      with Brunner TIMES WITHOUT NUMBER   Book: DESTINY'S ORBIT
   EDGE OF TIME   Ace   1958   145
      Book: same   with Brunner THE 100th MILLENNIUM
   THE MARTIAN MISSILE   Ace   1961   127
      with Brunner THE ATLANTIC ABOMINATION
Gruen, Von
   THE MORTALS OF RENI   Warren   1953   159
Gunn, James N.
   THE IMMORTALS   Bantam   1962   154
   THE JOYMAKERS   Bantam   1961   160
   STATION IN SPACE   Bantam   1958   156
   THIS FORTRESS WORLD   Ace   1957   190
      with Silverberg THE 13th IMMORTAL

Hadley, Arthur T.
   THE JOY WAGON   Berkley   1960   158
      Book: same
Hadley, Franklin
   PLANET BIG ZERO   Monarch   1964   126

Haggard, H. Rider
   ALLAN QUATERMAIN and
   KING SOLOMON'S MINES   Royal Books   nd   319
      Books: same Abr.
   BENITA   Chariot Books   London   1952   182
      Book: same
   SHE   Lancer   1961   256
      Book: same
Haley, Claud
   BEYOND THE SOLAR SYSTEM   Arc   London   1953   141
Hall, Austin
   THE SPOT OF LIFE   Ace   1965   187
Hall, Austin and Flint, Homer Eon
   THE BLIND SPOT   Ace   1964   318
      Book: same
Hamilton, Edmond
   BATTLE FOR THE STARS   Paperback Library   1964   159
      Book: same
   BEYOND THE MOON   Signet   1950   167
      Book: THE STAR KINGS
   THE CITY AT WORLD'S END   Fawcett   1961   160
      Book: same
   CRASHING SUNS   Ace   1965   192
   THE HAUNTED STARS   Pyramid   1960   159
      Book: same
   THE MONSTERS OF JUNTONHEIM   Pemberton   1950   160
   MURDER IN THE CLINIC   Utopia Pubn   nd   36
   OUTSIDE THE UNIVERSE   Ace   1964   173
   THE STAR OF LIFE   Fawcett   1959   187
      Book: same
   THARKOL, LORD OF THE UNKNOWN   Pemberton   1950   160
   TIGER GIRL   Utopia Pubn   nd   36
   THE VALLEY OF CREATION   Lancer   1964   159
   FUGITIVE OF THE STARS   Ace   1965   116
      with Bulmer LAND BEYOND THE MAP
   THE SUN SMASHER   Ace   1959   110
      with Jorgenson STARHAVEN
Hammett, Dashiell (Editor)
   CREEPS BY NIGHT   Belmont   1961   141
      Book: same Abr.
   THE RED BRAIN   Belmont   1961   141
      Book: part of CREEPS BY NIGHT
Harbou, Thea Von
   METROPOLIS   Ace   1963   222
      Book: same
Hardie, John L.
   SEVEN MORE STRANGE STORIES   Art & Educational   Glasgow   nd   80
Hardy, A. S.
   AZAR THE MIGHTY   Boys' Friend Library   1931   64
Hargrave, John
   THE IMITATION MAN   Gardner, Darton   London   1940   191
Harkon, Franz
   SPAWN OF SPACE   Scion, Ltd   1951   112

Harness, Charles L.
    THE PARADOX MEN   Ace   1955   133
        Book: FLIGHT INTO YESTERDAY   with Williamson DOME AROUND AMERICA
Harris, Johnson (Pseudonym of Harris, John Beynon)
    LOVE IN TIME   Utopia Pubn   nd   36
Harrison, Harry
    DEATHWORLD   Bantam   1960   154
    DEATHWORLD 2   Bantam   1964   151
    PLANET OF THE DAMNED   Bantam   1962   135
    THE STAINLESS STEEL RAT   Pyramid   1961   158
    WAR WITH THE ROBOTS   Pyramid   1962   158
Harvey, Robert E.
    MYORA; OR, THE LAND OF ETERNAL SUNSHINE   Gimlin Press   Chicago   1903   9
Hatch, Gerald
    THE DAY THE EARTH FROZE   Monarch   1963   125
Hatfull, J. D.
    IMPERIAL OVERTURE AND OTHER STORIES   Pictorial Art, Ltd   London   nd   32
Hawthorne, Julian
    A MESSENGER FROM THE UNKNOWN   Once A Week Library   1892   108
Hawthorne, Nathaniel
    THE MARBLE FAUN   Pocket Books   1958   388
        Book: same
    TWICE TOLD TALES   Pocket Books   1960   430
        Book: same
Hay, George
    FLIGHT OF THE "HESPER"   Hamilton   1951   112
    MAN, WOMAN--AND ANDROID   Hamilton   nd   108
    THIS PLANET FOR SALE   Hamilton   1951   111
Hayes, Jeff W.
    PORTLAND, OREGON, A. D. 1999 & OTHER SKETCHES   Baltes   Portland, Oregon
        1913   112
Healy, Raymond J. (Editor)
    NEW TALES OF SPACE AND TIME   Pocket Books   1958   273
        Book: same
Healy, Raymond J. and McComas, J. Francis (Editors)
    ADVENTURES IN TIME AND SPACE   Pennant Books   1954   200
        Book: selections from ADVENTURES IN TIME AND SPACE
    FAMOUS SCIENCE FICTION STORIES   Modern Library   1957   997
        Book: ADVENTURES IN TIME AND SPACE
    MORE ADVENTURES IN TIME AND SPACE   Bantam   1955   142
        Book: selections from ADVENTURES IN TIME AND SPACE
Heard, H. F.
    REPLY PAID   Dell   1943   237
        Book: same
    A TASTE FOR HONEY   Avon   1946   186
        Book: same
Hecht, Ben
    SELECTED GREAT STORIES   Avon   nd   164
Heinlein, Robert A.
    ASSIGNMENT IN ETERNITY   Signet   1954   192
        Book: same
    BETWEEN PLANETS   Scribner   1962   222
        Book: same

Heinlein, Robert A. (Cont.)
    THE DAY AFTER TOMORROW   Signet   1951   160
        Book: SIXTH COLUMN
    THE DOOR INTO SUMMER   Signet   1959   159
        Book: same
    DOUBLE STAR   Signet   1958   176
        Book: same
    THE GLORY ROAD   Avon   1964   194
        Book: same
    THE GREEN HILLS OF EARTH   Signet   1952   176
        Book: same
    THE MAN WHO SOLD THE MOON   Signet   1951   167
        Book: same
    THE MENACE FROM EARTH   Signet   1962   189
        Book: same
    METHUSELAH'S CHILDREN   Signet   1960   160
        Book: same
    ORPHANS OF THE SKY   Signet   1965   154
        Book: same
    PODKAYNE OF MARS   Avon   1964   159
        Book: same
    THE PUPPET MASTERS   Signet   1952   176
        Book: same
    REVOLT IN 2100   Signet   1955   192
        Book: same
    6 X H   Pyramid   1962   191
        Book: THE UNPLEASANT PROFESSION OF JONATHAN HOAG
    STARSHIP TROOPERS   Signet   1961   208
        Book: same
    UNIVERSE   Dell   1951   64
        Book: ORPHANS OF THE SKY first part
    WALDO AND MAGIC, INC.   Pyramid   1963   191
        Book: same
    WALDO: GENIUS IN ORBIT   Avon   1958   191
        Book: WALDO, AND MAGIC, INC.
Heinlein, Robert A. (Editor)
    TOMORROW, THE STARS   Signet   1953   207
        Book: same
Heming, J. W.
    IN AZTEC HANDS   Currawong   Sydney   1942   80
    KING OF THE UNDERSEAS   Currawong   Sydney   nd   64
    THE WEIRD HOUSE   Currawong   Sydney   1951   64
Henderson, Zenna
    PILGRIMAGE: THE BOOK OF THE PEOPLE   Avon   1964   255
        Book: same
Herbert, Benson
    HAND OF GLORY   Cole   London   nd   31
    THE RED HAIRED GIRL   Cole   London   nd   36
    STRANGE ROMANCE   Cole   London   nd   95
Herbert, Benson and Pragnell, Festus
    THIEVES OF THE AIR   Cole   London   nd   27
Herbert, Cyril
    THE MAN WHO WAS TEN YEARS LATE FOR BREAKFAST   Pillar   Dublin   nd   79
    HOW SLOW THE SMOOTH   Pillar   Dublin   nd   78

Herbert, Frank
   21st CENTURY SUB   Avon   1959   190
      Book: THE DRAGON IN THE SEA
Hervey, Michael
   HORROR MEDLEY   The Hampton Press   Essex, England   nd   32
   QUEER LOOKING BOX   Everybody's Books   nd   32
   STRANGE HUNGER   nd   128
Hesse, Herman
   MAGISTER LUDI   Ungar Paperbacks   1957   502
      Book: THE BEAD GAME
   STEPPENWOLF   Ungar Paperbacks   1957   300
      Book: same
High, Philip E.
   THE PRODIGAL SUN   Ace   1964   192
   NO TRUCE WITH TERRA   Ace   1964   110
      with Leinster THE DUPLICATORS
Hilton, James
   LOST HORIZON   Pocket Books   1939   169
      Book: same
Hitchcock, Alfred (Editor)
   BAR THE DOORS!   Dell   1946   192
   FEAR AND TREMBLING   Dell   1948   192
   HOLD YOUR BREATH   Dell   1947   192
   ONCE UPON A DREADFUL TIME   Dell   1964   192
   SUSPENSE STORIES   Dell   1949   192
   12 STORIES FOR LATE AT NIGHT   Dell   1963   223
      Book: same
   12 STORIES THEY WOULDN'T LET ME DO ON T V   Dell   1958   224
      Book: STORIES THEY WOULDN'T LET ME DO ON T V first part
   13 MORE STORIES THEY WOULDN'T LET ME DO ON T V   Dell   1959   224
      Book: STORIES THEY WOULDN'T LET ME DO ON T V second part
   14 OF MY FAVORITES IN SUSPENSE   Dell   1960   288
      Book: same
   MORE OF MY FAVORITES IN SUSPENSE   Dell   1961   287
      Book: same
Hodgson, William Hope
   THE HOUSE ON THE BORDERLAND   Ace   1961   157
      Book: same (not the omnibus Arkham House edition)
Hogg, James
   THE PRIVATE MEMOIRS AND CONFESSIONS OF A JUSTIFIED SINNER   Grove Press
      1959   230
      Book: same
Holbert, Ludvig
   JOURNEY OF NIELS KLIM TO THE WORLD UNDERGROUND   University of Nebraska Press
      Lincoln   1960   236
      Book: same
Holden, Richard
   SNOW FURY   Permabooks   1956   194
      Book: same
Holland, W. Bob
   THE PERMA BOOK OF GHOST STORIES   Permabooks   1950   188
Holly, J. Hunter
   ENCOUNTER   Monarch   1962   142
      Book: same

Holly, J. Hunter (Cont.)
    THE FLYING EYES   Monarch   1962   140
    THE GREEN PLANET   Monarch   1961   143
    THE RUNNING MAN   Monarch   1963   142
    THE TIME TWISTERS   Avon   1965   176
Holt, Conrad G.
    COSMIC EXODUS   Pearson   London   nd   64
Home-Gall, Edward R.
    THE HUMAN BAT   Mark Goulden   London   nd   127
    THE HUMAN BAT V THE ROBOT GANGSTER   Mark Goulden   London   nd   128
Hopkins, R. Thurston
    HORROR PARADE   Mitre Press   nd   63
    UNCANNY TALES   Mitre Press   nd   32
    WEIRD AND UNCANNY STORIES   Mitre Press   nd   32
Hopley, George
    THE NIGHT HAS A THOUSAND EYES   Dell   nd   288
        Book: same
Horan, Keith
    THE SQUID   Bernardo Amalgamated   London   nd   64
Horler, Sidney
    VIRUS X   Archer Press   London   1950   126
        Book: same
Houghton, Claude
    CHAOS IS COME AGAIN   Penguin   1932   311
    THE MAN WHO COULD STILL LAUGH   Bantam Books   London   1943   16
Household, Geoffrey
    THE SPANISH CAVE   Comet Books   1948   178
        Book: same
Howard, Ivan (Editor)
    ESCAPE TO EARTH   Belmont   1963   173
    NOVELETS OF SCIENCE FICTION   Belmont   1963   173
    6 AND THE SILENT SCREAM   Belmont   1963   173
    THINGS   Belmont   1964   157
    WAY OUT   Belmont   1963   173
Howard, M. W.
    IF CHRIST CAME TO CONGRESS   Howard Pub Co   Washington, D. C.   1894
Howard, Robert E.
    ALMURIC   Ace   1964   157·
Howard, Robert E. and Others
    THE GARDEN OF FEAR   Crawford   Los Angeles   1945   79
Howard, Robert E.
    CONAN THE CONQUEROR   Ace   1953   116
        Book: same   with Brackett SWORD OF RHIANNON
Hoyle, Fred
    THE BLACK CLOUD   Signet   1959   190
        Book: same
    OSSIAN'S RIDE   Berkley   1961   153
        Book: same
Hubbard, L. Ron
    FEAR   Galaxy Novel   1957   125
        Book: TYPEWRITER IN THE SKY and FEAR second part
    RETURN TO TOMORROW   Ace   1954   157
    TYPEWRITER IN THE SKY and FEAR   Kensley Newspapers   London   1952   190
        Book: same

Hudson, W. H.
  GREEN MANSIONS Bantam 1946 297
    Book: same
Hughes, Denis
  THE EARTH INVASION BATTALION Warren nd 128
  FORMULA 695 Warren nd 128
  MOON WAR Warren nd 128
  MURDER BY TELECOPTER Warren nd 127
  WAR LORDS OF SPACE Warren nd 128
Hughes, Dorothy
  THE DELICATE APE Armed Forces edition nd 137
    Book: same
Hunt, Gill
  ELEKTRON UNION Warren nd 112
  FISSION Warren 1950 111
  GALACTIC STORM Warren 1952 110
  HOSTILE WORLDS Warren nd 112
  PLANET X Warren nd 112
  PLANETFALL Warren 1952 111
  SPACE FLIGHT Warren nd 111
  SPATIAL RAY Warren nd 111
  STATION 7 Warren 1951 112
  VEGA Warren nd 111
  ZERO FIELD Warren nd 112
Huxley, Aldous
  AFTER MANY A SUMMER DIES THE SWAN Avon nd 254
    Book: same
  APE AND ESSENCE Bantam 1958 152
    Book: same
  BRAVE NEW WORLD Bantam 1953 177
    Book: same
  BRAVE NEW WORLD REVISITED Bantam 1960 116
    Book: same
  EYELESS IN GAZA Bantam 1963 423
    Book: same
  POINT COUNTER POINT Avon nd 444
    Book: same
  TIME MUST HAVE A STOP Berkley 1957 239
    Book: same

Inca-Pancho-Ozollo
  THE LOST INCA Cassell London 1889 286
Irving, Washington
  THE LEGEND OF SLEEPY HOLLOW Airmont 1964 190
    Book: same

Jackson, Shirley
  THE SUNDIAL Ace 1962 192
    Book: same
James, Henry
  THE TURN OF THE SCREW Dell 1954 191
    Book: same

James, M. R.
　GHOST STORIES OF AN ANTIQUARY　Penguin　1937　152
　　　Book:　same
　MORE GHOST STORIES　Penguin　1959　154
　　　Book:　same
　A THIN GHOST　Penguin　1961　152
　　　Book:　same
Jameson, Malcolm
　ATOMIC BOMB　Bond Charteris Pub　Los Angeles　1945　128
　TARNISHED UTOPIA　Galaxy Novel　1956　126
Janifer, Laurence M.
　SLAVE PLANET　Pyramid　1963　148
　THE WONDER WAR　Pyramid　1964　127
　YOU SAME MEN　Lancer　1965　159
Jenkins, Will F.
　DESTROY THE U. S. A.　News Stand Library　Toronto　1950　157
　　　Book:　THE MURDER OF THE U. S. A.
　THE SOLDADO ANT　Malian Press　Sydney　1951　34
Jones, Guy and Constance
　PEABODY'S MERMAID　Pocket Books　1948　184
　　　Book:　same
Jones, Raymond F.
　THE ALIEN　Galaxy Novel　1951　160
　THE DEVIATES　Galaxy Novel　1959　160
　　　Book:　THE SECRET PEOPLE
　MAN OF TWO WORLDS　Pyramid　1963　268
　　　Book:　RENAISSANCE
　THE NON-STATISTICAL MAN　Belmont　1964　158
Jorgensen, Ivar
　REST IN AGONY　Monarch　1963　125
　STARHAVEN　Ace　1959　146
　　　Book:　same　with Hamilton THE SUN SMASHER
　TEN FROM INFINITY　Monarch　1963　139
Joyce, (Col.) John A.
　NAZER (A ZIGZAG PHILOSOPHY)　Universal Pub Co　Chicago　1893　187
Judd, Cyril
　OUTPOST MARS　Dell　1952　223
　　　Book:　same
　SIN IN SPACE　Beacon (Galaxy Novel)　1961　190
　　　Book:　OUTPOST MARS (more or less)
　GUNNER CADE　Ace　1957　198
　　　Book:　same　with Piper CRISIS IN 2140
Juenger, Ernst
　THE GLASS BEES　Noonday Press　1961　149
　　　Book:　same

Kaner, Human
　APE-MAN'S OFFERING　Kaner　Llandudno, Wales　nd　64
　FIRE WATCHER'S NIGHT　Kaner　Llandudno, Wales　nd　56
　HOT SWAG　Brown, Watson　London　nd　64
　THE NAKED FOOT　Kaner　Llandudno, Wales　nd　64
　ORDEAL BY MOONLIGHT　Kaner　Llandudno, Wales　nd　64
　SQUARING THE TRIANGLE AND OTHER SHORT STORIES　Kaner　Llandudno, Wales
　　　nd　64

Kantor, MacKinley
    IF THE SOUTH HAD WON THE CIVIL WAR   Bantam   1961   113
Kapp, Colin
    TRANSFINITE MAN   Berkley   1964   160
Karlova, Irina
    DREADFUL HOLLOW   Dell   1948   240
        Book: same
Karp, David
    ESCAPE TO NOWHERE   Lion Books   1954   124
        Book: ONE
Keene, Day and Pruyn, Leonard
    WORLD WITHOUT WOMEN   Fawcett   1960   160
Kellar, Von
    IONIC BARRIER   Warren   1953   159
        Book: same
    TRI-PLANET   Warren   1953   159
Kelleam, Joseph
    OVERLORDS FROM SPACE   Ace   1956   146
        with Cummings THE MAN WHO MASTERED TIME
Keller, David H.
    FIGMENT OF A DREAM   Chalker   Baltimore   1962   39
    THE FINAL WAR   Perri Press   Portland, Oregon   1949   21
    THE TELEVISION DETECTIVE   LASFL   Los Angeles   1938   13
    WATERS OF LETHE   Kirby   Great Barrington, Mass.   1937   no pagination
    MEN OF AVALON   Fantasy Pub Co   Everett, Pa.   nd
        with Smith THE WHITE SIBYL   38 pages
Kelley, Thomas P.
    THE FACE THAT LAUNCHED A THOUSAND SHIPS   Adam Pub Co   Toronto   1941   125
Kennedy, Edgar Rees
    CONQUERORS OF VENUS   Self   nd   128
    THE MYSTERY PLANET   Self   1952   128
Kennerley, Juba
    THE TERROR OF THE LEOPARD MEN   Avon   1951   192
Kensch, Otto
    IMAGE OF DEATH   Transport Pub Co   1950   49
    SLEEP IS DEATH   Transport Pub Co   1948   50
    TIME HAS A DOOR   Transport Pub Co   1950   50
Kent, Brad
    BIOLOGY "A"   Warren   1952   128
    CATALYST   Warren   1951   112
    THE FATAL LAW   Warren   nd   112
    OUT OF THE SILENT PLACES   Warren   1952   127
Kent, Philip
    MISSION TO THE STARS   Pearson   London   1954   64
Kerr, Geoffrey
    UNDER THE INFLUENCE   Berkley   1961   189
        Book: same
Kersh, Gerald
    THE BATTLE OF THE SINGING MEN   Staples & Staples   London   1944   61
    MEN WITHOUT BONES   Paperback Library   1962   223
        Book: same
    ON AN ODD NOTE   Ballantine   1958   154
    THE SECRET MASTERS   Ballantine   1953   225
        Book: same

King, John
 SHUNA AND THE LOST TRIBE Harborough Pub Co Stoke-on-Trent, England
  1951 128
 SHUNA, WHITE QUEEN OF THE JUNGLE Harborough Pub Co Stoke-on-Trent, England
  1951 128
Kinley, George
 FERRY ROCKET Warren 1954 159
Kinson, Nixon
 TERROR ABOVE THE STRATOSPHERE Barton London nd 32
Kipling, Rudyard
 THE JUNGLE BOOKS Signet 1961 332
  Book: same
Kirk, H. C.
 WHEN AGE GROWS YOUNG Dillingham 1888 281
Kirst, Hans Helmut
 THE SEVENTH DAY Ace nd 383
  Book: same
Kline, Otis Adelbert
 THE MALIGNANT ENTITY Utopia Pubn nd 36
 THE MAN WHO LIMPED Saint Hollywood 1946 128
 MAZA OF THE MOON Ace 1965 144
  Book: same
 OUTLAWS OF MARS Ace 1962 158
  Book: same
 PLANET OF PERIL Ace 1962 160
  Book: same
 THE PORT OF PERIL Ace 1964 192
  Book: same
 THE PRINCE OF PERIL Ace 1964 174
  Book: same
 THE SWORDSMAN OF MARS Ace 1961 174
  Book: same
Kneale, Nigel
 THE QUATERMASS EXPERIMENT Penguin 1959 192
 QUATERMASS II Penguin 1960 172
 QUATERMASS AND THE PIT Penguin 1960 188
Knight, Damon
 ANALOGUE MEN Berkley 1963 160
  original title: HELL'S PAVEMENT
 BEYOND THE BARRIER Macfadden-Bartell 1964 154
 HELL'S PAVEMENT Lion Books 1955 192
 IN DEEP Berkley 1963 158
 OFF CENTER Ace 1965 141
  with THE RITHIAN TERROR Ace 1965 111
 THE PEOPLE MAKER Zenith 1959 159
Knight, Damon (Editor)
 A CENTURY OF SCIENCE FICTION Dell 1963 284
  Book: same
 FAR OUT Berkley 1962 192
  Book: same
 FIRST FLIGHT: MAIDEN VOYAGES IN SPACE AND TIME Lancer 1963 160
 THE SHAPE OF THINGS Popular Library 1965 166
Knight, Damon
 MASTERS OF EVOLUTION Ace 1959 96
  with Smith FIRE IN THE HEAVENS

Knight, Damon (Cont.)
    THE SUN SABOTEURS   Ace   1961   101
        with Wallis LIGHT OF LILITH
Knight, Eric
    THE FLYING YORKSHIREMAN   Pocket Books   1948   273
        Book: SAM SMALL FLIES AGAIN
Knox, Calvin
    LEST WE FORGET THEE, EARTH   Ace   1958   126
        with Gallun PEOPLE MINUS X
    ONE OF OUR ASTEROIDS IS MISSING   Ace   1964   124
        with van Vogt THE TWISTED MEN
    THE PLOT AGAINST EARTH   Ace   1959   138
        with Lesser RECRUIT FOR ANDROMEDA
Kornbluth, Cyril M.
    THE EXPLORERS   Ballantine   1954   145
    THE MARCHING MORONS   Ballantine   1959   158
    A MILE BEYOND THE MOON   Macfadden-Bartell   1962   175
        Book: same
    NOT THIS AUGUST   Bantam   1956   165
        Book: same
    THE SYNDIC   Bantam   1955   142
        Book: same
    TAKEOFF   Pennant Books   1953   149
        Book: same
Kramer, Nora (Editor)
    ARROW BOOK OF GHOST STORIES   Scholastic Book Service   1960   116
Kummer, F. A.
    LADIES IN HADES   Dell   1952   158
        Book: same
Kuttner, Henry
    AHEAD OF TIME   Ballantine   1953   179
        Book: same
    BYPASS TO OTHERNESS   Ballantine   1961   144
    THE DARK WORLD   Ace   1965   126
    DESTINATION: INFINITY   Avon   1959   192
        Book: FURY
    MUTANT   Ballantine   1963   191
        Book: same - under pseudonym of Lewis Padgett
    RETURN TO OTHERNESS   Ballantine   1962   240
    VALLEY OF THE FLAME   Ace   1964   156
Kuttner, Henry and Moore, C. L.
    NO BOUNDARIES   Ballantine   1955   151
        Book: same

La Salle, Victor
    AFTER THE ATOM   Spencer   nd   108
    ASSAULT FROM INFINITY   Spencer   1953   108
    THE BLACK SPHERE   Spencer   nd   108
    DAWN OF THE HALF-GODS   Spencer   1953   128
    THE 7th DIMENSION   Spencer   1953   124
    SUNS IN DUO   Spencer   nd   108
Laing, Alexander
    THE CADAVER OF GIDEON WYCK   Collier   1962   250
        Book: same Abr.

Leiber, Fritz (Cont.)
    DESTINY TIMES THREE   Galaxy Novel   1957   126
    GATHER, DARKNESS   Berkley   1963   174
        Book: same
    THE GREEN MILLENNIUM   Lion Books   1954   124
        Book: same
    NIGHT'S BLACK AGENTS   Ballantine   1961   143
        Book: same Abr.
    A PAIL OF AIR   Ballantine   1964   191
    SHADOWS WITH EYES   Ballantine   1962   128
    THE SILVER EGGHEADS   Ballantine   1961   192
    THE WANDERER   Ballantine   1964   318
    SHIPS TO THE STARS   Ace   1964   122
        with Bulmer THE MILLION YEAR HUNT
Leinster, Murray
    THE ALIENS   Berkley   1960   144
    THE BLACK GALAXY   Galaxy Novel   1954   126
    CONQUEST OF THE STARS   Malian Press   Sydney   1951   34
    CREATURES OF THE ABYSS   Berkley   1961   143
    DOCTOR TO THE STARS   Pyramid   1964   178
    FIGHT FOR LIFE   Crestwood   1949   118
    FOUR FROM PLANET FIVE   Fawcett   1959   160
    THE GREEKS BRING GIFTS   Macfadden-Bartell   1964   176
    INVADERS OF SPACE   Berkley   1964   144
    THE LAST SPACE SHIP   Galaxy Novel   1955   126
        Book: same
    MEN INTO SPACE   Berkely   1961   142
    THE MONSTER FROM EARTH'S END   Fawcett   1959   176
    MONSTERS AND SUCH   Avon   1960   141
    OPERATION: OUTER SPACE   Fantasy Press   Reading, Pa.   1954   203
        Book: same
    OPERATION TERROR   Berkley   1962   160
    THE OTHER SIDE OF NOWHERE   Berkley   1964   142
    THE PIRATES OF ZAN   Ace   1960   163
        with THE MUTANT WEAPON   Ace   1960   93
    THE PLANET EXPLORER   Avon   1957   171
        Book: COLONIAL SURVEY
    SPACE PLATFORM   Pocket Books   1953   157
        Book: same
    SPACE TUG   Pocket Books   1955   154
        Book: same
    TALENTS, INC.   Avon   1962   159
    THIS WORLD IS TABOO   Ace   1961   127
    TIME TUNNEL   Pyramid   1964   140
    TWISTS IN TIME   Avon   1960   160
    THE WAILING ASTEROID   Avon   1960   143
    WAR WITH THE GIZMOS   Fawcett   1958   156
    THE BRAIN STEALERS   Ace   1954   124
        with Bellamy ATTA
    CITY ON THE MOON   Ace   1958   151
        Book: same   with Wollheim MEN ON THE MOON
    THE DUPLICATORS   Ace   1964   143
        with High NO TRUCE WITH TERRA

Leinster, Murray (Cont.)
    THE FORGOTTEN PLANET   Ace   1956   143
      Book: same   with Correy CONTRABAND ROCKET
    GATEWAY TO ELSEWHERE   Ace   1954   134
      with van Vogt THE WEAPON SHOPS OF ISHER
    THE OTHER SIDE OF HERE   Ace   1955   144
      with van Vogt ONE AGAINST ETERNITY
Lengyel, Cornel
    THE ATOM CLOCK   Fantasy Pub Co   Los Angeles   1951   66   Play
Leroux, Gaston
    THE PHANTOM OF THE OPERA   Dell   New York   nd   239
      Book: same
Lesser, Milton
    RECRUIT FOR ANDROMEDA   Ace   1959   117
      with Knox THE PLOT AGAINST EARTH
Lester, H(orace) F.
    HARTAS MATURIN; A NOVEL   Lovell   1889   404
Levis, Rex Dean
    THE INSECT WARRIORS   Ace   1965   143
Lewis, C. S.
    OUT OF THE SILENT PLANET   Avon   1949   159
      Book: same
    PERELANDRA   Avon   1950   191
      Book: same
    THAT HIDEOUS STRENGTH   Collier   1962   382
      Book: same
    TILL WE HAVE FACES   Eerdman   1964   313
      Book: same
    THE TORTURED PLANET   Avon   1952   254
      Book: THAT HIDEOUS STRENGTH Abr.
    VOYAGE TO VENUS   Pan Books   1954   159
      Book: PERELANDRA
Lewis, Irwin
    THE DAY THEY INVADED NEW YORK   Avon   1964   160
Lewis, Sinclair
    IT CAN'T HAPPEN HERE   Dell   1961   382
      Book: same
Lincoln, Maurice
    THE MAN FROM SPACE   Boys' Friend Library   1932   95
Lindner, Robert
    THE FIFTY MINUTE HOUR   Bantam   1956   207
      Book: same
Lippard, George
    THE MYSTERIES OF FLORENCE   Peterson's   Philadelphia   1964   233
Livingston, Harold
    THE CLIMACTICON   Ballantine   1960   191
Locke, Richard Adams
    THE MOON HOAX   Gowans   1859   63
Long, Frank Belknap
    THE DARK BEASTS   Belmont   1964   141
      Book: THE HOUNDS OF TINDALOS selections
    THE GOBLIN TOWER   New Collectors   Denver   1949   30
    THE HORROR EXPERT   Belmont   1961   141

Long, Frank Belknap (Cont.)
    THE HOUNDS OF TINDALOS   Belmont   1963   173
      Book: same - selections
    IT WAS THE DAY OF THE ROBOT   Belmont   1963   141
    JOHN CARSTAIRS, SPACE DETECTIVE   Kemsley Newspapers   London   1951   192
      Book: same
    MARS IS MY DESTINATION   Pyramid   1962   158
    ODD SCIENCE FICTION   Belmont   1964   141
      Book: THE HORROR FROM THE HILLS
    SPACE STATION #1   Ace   1957   157
      with van Vogt EMPIRE OF THE ATOM
Loomis, Noel
    CITY OF GLASS   Columbia Pubn   1955   128
Lorraine, Paul
    DARK BOUNDARIES   Warren   1953   159
    TWO WORLDS   Warren   1952   128
    ZENITH-D   Warren   1952   159
Lounsberry, (Lieut.) Lionel
    THE TREASURE OF THE GOLDEN CRATER   Street & Smith   1928   248
Louys, Pierre
    APHRODITE   Berkley   1959   158
      Book: same
Lovecraft, H. P.
    THE CASE OF CHARLES DEXTER WARD   Belmont   1965   155
      Book: same
    THE COLOUR OUT OF SPACE   Lancer   1964   222
      Book: part of THE OUTSIDER
    THE DREAM QUEST OF UNKNOWN KADATH   Shroud   Buffalo   1955   107
      Book: same
    CRY HORROR   Avon   1957   191
      Original title THE LURKING FEAR
    THE DUNWICH HORROR   Armed Services Editions   nd   384
    THE DUNWICH HORROR   Lancer   1963   158
      Book: same Abr.
    THE LURKING FEAR   Avon   1947   223
      Book: part of THE OUTSIDER
    THE WEIRD SHADOW OVER INNSMOUTH   Bartholomew House   1944   190
      Book: same
Lovecraft, H. P. and Derleth, August
    THE SURVIVOR AND OTHERS   Ballantine   1961   143
      Book: same
Lowndes, Marie Belloc
    THE LODGER   Pocket Books   1940   243
      Book: same
Lowndes, Robert A. W.
    THE PUZZLE PLANET   Ace   1961   119
      with Biggle THE ANGRY ESPERS
Lucky, Robert Motford
    THE DEVIL WORSHIPPERS   Neely   1898   280
Ludwig, Boris
    JAWS OF DEATH   Cresta   Sydney   nd   50
Luigi, Belli
    CRIME FLIES   Transport Pub Co   1947   50
    DEATH HAS NO WEIGHT   Transport Pub Co   1947   50

Luigi, Bolli (Cont.)
    DEPTHS OF DEATH   Transport Pub Co   nd   50
    THE FREEZING PERIL STRIKES   Transport Pub Co   1949   34
    THE GLOWING GLOBE   Transpost Pub Co   1948   50
    THE LOST UNDERWORLD   Transport Pub Co   1948   50
    MASTER-MIND MENACE   Pemberton   1950   128
    THE METAL MONSTER   Pemberton   1950   128
Luna, Kris
    OPERATION ORBIT   Warren   1953   159
    STELLA RADIUM DISCHARGE   Warren   1952   128
        Book: same
Lynn, Grey
    THE RETURN OF KARL MARX   Chancery Books   London   1941   117
Lyttleton, Lord
    DIALOGUES OF THE DEAD   Cassell   London and New York   1889   192

Macardle, Dorothy
    THE UNFORSEEN   Bantam   1951   279
        Book: same
    THE UNINVITED   Bantam   1947   341
        Book: same
Macartney, Clem
    DARK SIDE OF VENUS   Hamilton   nd   111
    TEN YEARS TO OBLIVION   Hamilton   nd   109
MacDonald John D.
    PLANET OF THE DREAMERS   Pocket Books   1953   164
        Book: WINE OF THE DREAMERS
MacDonald, George
    PHANTASIES & LILITH   Eerdmans   1964   420
        Books: same
Machen, Arthur
    HOLY TERRORS   Penguin   nd   140
    THE STRANGE WORLD OF ARTHUR MACHEN   Juniper Press   nd   381
        Books: THE THREE IMPOSTORS, THE GREAT GOD PAN, THE SHINING PYRAMID, etc.
MacLean, Katherine
    THE DIPLOIDS   Avon   1962   192
Macrae, Herbert
    THE INVISIBLE AVENGER   Champion Library   1936   63
Maddox, Carl
    THE LIVING WORLD   Pearson   London   1954   64
MacTyre, Paul
    DOOMSDAY, 1999   Ace   1962   158
    MENACE FROM THE PAST   Pearson   London   1954   64
Magroon, Vector
    BURNING VOID   Scion, Ltd   1952   128
Maine, Charles Eric
    FIRE PAST THE FUTURE   Ballantine   1959   160
    HE OWNED THE WORLD   Avon   1960   144
        Book: same
    HIGH VACUUM   Ballantine   1957   185
        Book: same
    SPACEWAYS   Pan Books   1955   160
        Book: SPACEWAYS SATELLITE
    THE TIDE WENT OUT   Ballantine   1959   156

Maine, Charles Eric (Cont.)
    TIMELINER   Bantam   1956   182
        Book: same
    WORLD WITHOUT MEN   Ace   1958   190
Mair, George B.
    THE DAY KRUSCHEV PANICKED   Macfadden-Bertall   1963   159
        Book: same
Malcolm, Grant
    THE GREEN MANDARIN MYSTERY   Warren   nd   127
Malcolm-Smith, George
    THE GRASS IS ALWAYS GREENER   Bantam   1948   184
        Book: same
Mannheim, Karl
    VAMPIRES OF VENUS   Pemberton   1952   128
    WHEN THE EARTH DIED   Pemberton   1950   128
Mannon, Warwick
    MIRANDA   World Film Pubn   London   1948   78
Mantley, John
    THE 27th DAY   Fawcett   1958   176
        Book: same
Maras, Karl
    PERIL FROM SPACE   Comyns, Ltd   London   1954   128
    ZHORANI   Comuns, Ltd   London   1953   128
Margulies, Leo (Editor)
    GET OUT OF MY SKY   Fawcett   1960   176
    THE GHOUL KEEPERS   Pyramid   1961   157
    3 FROM OUT THERE   Fawcett   1959   192
    3 TIMES INFINITY   Fawcett   1958   176
    THE UNEXPECTED   Pyramid   1961   160
    WEIRD TALES   Pyramid   1964   155
Margulies, Leo and Friend, Oscar J. (Editors)
    MY BEST SCIENCE FICTION STORY   Pocket Books   1954   263
        Book: same Abr.
    RACE TO THE STARS   Fawcett   1958   224
        Book: 4 stories from GIANT ANTHOLOGY OF SCIENCE FICTION
Marks, Simon
    DOWN AMAZON WAY   Pocket Editions   London   nd   16
Marlowe, Gabriel
    CHEZ ROBERT AND OTHER ROMANCES   Utopia Pubn   nd   44
Marquis, Don
    ARCHY AND MEHITABEL   Faber   London   1958   166
        Book: same
Marquis, Roy
    THE MOON MONSTERS   Gray   Leigh-on-sea, Essex, England   nd   128
Marriott, Crittenden
    THE WATER DEVIL   Garden City Pub Co   1924   117
Marsh, Richard
    THE APE AND THE DIAMOND   Street & Smith   1928   320
Marshall, Edison
    THE DEATH BELL   Garden City Pub Co   1924   120
Martin, Stuart
    WHEN THE GREAT APES CAME   Boys' Friend Library   1935   86
Matheson, Richard
    I AM LEGEND   Fawcett   1954   160

Matheson, Richard (Cont.)
    SHOCK   Dell   1961   191
    SHOCK II   Dell   1964   164
    THE SHORES OF SPACE   Bantam   1957   184
    THE SHRINKING MAN   Fawcett   1956   192
    A STIR OF ECHOES   Fawcett   1959   175
        Book: same
    THIRD FROM THE SUN   Bantam   1955   180
        Book: BORN OF MAN AND WOMAN Abr.
Maturin, Charles Robert
    MELMOTH THE WANDERER   University of Nebraska Press   Lincoln   1961   412
        Book: same
Maugham, Robin
    THE 1946 MS.   The War Facts Press   London   1943   44
Maugham, W. Somerset
    COSMOPOLITANS   Berkley   1959   157
        Book: same
    THE MAGICIAN   Pocket Books   1958   209
        Book: same
Maxon, P. B.
    THE WALTZ OF DEATH   Bartholomew House   1944   18 8
Maxwell, Jack
    TERROR FROM THE STRATOSPHERE   Champion Library   1937   64
McCowan, Archibald
    THE BILLIONAIRE; A PEEP INTO THE FUTURE   Jenkins & McCowan   1900   79
McCann, Edson
    PREFERRED RISK   Dell   1962   190
        Book: same
McClary, Thomas Calvert
    REBIRTH - WHEN EVERYONE FORGOT   Bartholomew House   1944   187
    3 THOUSAND YEARS   Ace   1956   128
        Book: THREE THOUSAND YEARS - a new version of REBIRTH
        with St. Clair THE GREEN QUEEN
McDougle, William
    THE FEMALE DEMON   Shroud Pub   Buffalo   1955   76   poetry
McHugh, Vincent
    I AM THINKING OF MY DARLING   Signet   1950   224
        Book: same
McInnes, Graham
    LOST ISLAND   Signet   1955   191
        Book: same
McIntosh, J. T.
    THE MILLION CITIES   Pyramid   1963   141
    THE RULE OF THE PAGBEASTS   Fawcett   1956   192
        Book: THE FITTEST
    WORLD OUT OF MIND   Pocket Books   1956   166
        Book: same
    WORLDS APART   Avon   1958   189
        Book: BORN LEADER
    ONE IN 300   Ace   1955   222
        Book: ONE IN THREE HUNDRED   with Swain THE TRANSPOSED MAN
    200 YEARS TO CHRISTMAS   Ace   1961   81
        with Fontenay REBELS OF THE RED PLANET
McLaren, Jack
    STORIES OF FEAR   Pendulum   London   nd   64

McLaughlin, Dean
    DOME WORLD   Pyramid   1962   159
    THE FURY FROM EARTH   Pyramid   1963   192
    THE MAN WHO WANTED STARS   Lancer   1965   156
Mead, Harold
    THE BRIGHT PHOENIX   Ballantine   1956   184
        Book: same
Mead, Shepherd
    THE BIG BALL OF WAX   Ballantine   1954   182
        Book: same
Meek, (Major) S. P.
    ARCTIC BRIDE   Utopia Pubn   nd   36
Melde, G. R.
    PACIFIC ADVANCE   Warren   1954   159
Menen, Aubrey
    THE PREVALENCE OF WITCHES   Scribner   1961   271
        Book: same
Merak, A. J.
    BARRIER UNKNOWN   Badger   nd   158
    DARK CONFLICT   Badger   nd   158
    DARK ANDROMEDA   Hamilton   1954   159
    THE LONELY SHADOWS   Badger   nd   158
    NO DAWN AND NO HORIZON   Badger   nd   158
    SOMETHING ABOUT SPIDERS   Badger   nd   158
Merril, Judith
    THE TOMORROW PEOPLE   Pyramid   1960   192
Merril, Judith (Editor)
    BEYOND HUMAN KEN   Pennant Books   1954   248
        Book: same Abr.
    GALAXY OF GHOULS   Lion Books   1955   192
    HUMAN?   Lion Books   1954   190
    OFF THE BEATEN ORBIT   Pyramid   1959   192
        Original title GALAXY OF GHOULS
    OUT OF BOUNDS   Pyramid   1960   160
    S F; THE YEAR'S GREATEST SCIENCE FICTION AND FANTASY   Dell   1956   290
        Book: same
    S F; THE YEAR'S GREATEST SCIENCE FICTION AND FANTASY 2nd Annual Volume
        Dell   1957   268
        Book: same
    S F; THE YEAR'S GREATEST SCIENCE FICTION AND FANTASY 3rd Annual Volume
        Dell   1958   255
        Book: S F: '58
    S F; THE YEAR'S GREATEST SCIENCE FICTION AND FANTASY 4th Annual Volume
        Dell   1959   256
        Book: S F: '59
    THE 5th ANNUAL OF THE YEAR'S BEST S F   Dell   1961   340
        Book: same
    THE 6th ANNUAL OF THE YEAR'S BEST S F   Dell   1962   362
        Book: same
    7th ANNUAL EDITION THE YEAR'S BEST S F   Dell   1963   399
        Book: same
    8th ANNUAL EDITION THE YEAR'S BEST S F   Dell   1964   328
        Book: same
    9th ANNUAL EDITION THE YEAR'S BEST S F   Dell   1965   284
        Book: same

Merril, Judith (Editor) (Cont.)
    SHOT IN THE DARK   Bantam   1950   308
Merritt, A.
    BURN WITCH, BURN   Avon   1942   223
        Book: same
    CREEP, SHADOW, CREEP   Avon   1943   255
        Book: CREEP, SHADOW
    DWELLERS IN THE MIRAGE   Avon   1944   158
        Book: same
    THE FACE IN THE ABYSS   Avon   1945   205
        Book: same
    THE FOX WOMAN   Avon   1949   157
        Book: same (this was finished by Hannes Bok) - plus selected short stories
    THE METAL MONSTER   Avon   1946   203
    THE MOON POOL   Avon   1944   201
        Book: same
    SEVEN FOOTPRINTS TO SATAN   Avon   1942   310
        Book: same
    THE SHIP OF ISHTAR   Avon   1945   168
        Book: same
Merwin, Sam, Jr.
    THE HOUSE OF MANY WORLDS   Galaxy Novel   1952   126
        Book: same
    KILLER TO COME   Galaxy Novel   1954   126
        Book: same
    THE SEX WAR   Beacon (Galaxy Novel)   1960   160
        Book: THE WHITE WIDOWS
    THREE FACES OF TIME   Ace   1955   135
        with Norton THE STARS ARE OURS
Niall, Derwent
    THE "DIVING DUCK"   Henderson   London   nd   93
Millard, Joseph
    THE GODS HATE KANSAS   Monarch   1964   126
Miller, George N.
    THE STRIKE OF A SEX   Dillingham   1890   235
Miller, R. DeWitt and Hunger, Anne
    THE MAN WHO LIVED FOREVER   Ace   1956   137
        with Sohl THE MARS MONOPOLY
Miller, Sutro
    "H" FOR HORRIFIC   Sentinel   London   1947   80
Miller, Walter, M., Jr.
    A CANTICLE FOR LEIBOWITZ   Bantam   1961   278
        Book: same
    CONDITIONALLY HUMAN   Ballantine   1962   191
    THE VIEW FROM THE STARS   Ballantine   1965   192
Mills, Robert P. (Editor)
    THE BEST FROM FANTASY AND SCIENCE FICTION 9th Series   Ace   1964   256
        Book: same
    THE BEST FROM FANTASY AND SCIENCE FICTION Tenth Series   Ace   1965   252
        Book: same
Mistral, Bengo
    THE BRAINS OF HELLE   Gannet Press   1953   127
    PIRATES OF CEREBUS   Gannet Press   1953   128
    SPACE FLIGHT 139   Gannet Press   nd   128

Mitchell, J. Leslie
 THREE GO BACK Galaxy Novel 1953 126
  Book: same
Molesworth, Vol
 THE APE OF GOD Currawong Pub Co Sydney nd 64
 SPACEWARD HO! Transport Pub Co nd 50
 THE STRATOSPHERE PATROL Transport Pub Co nd 48
 THE THREE ROCKETEERS Transport Pub Co nd 50
Moore, C. L.
 DOOMSDAY MORNING Avon 1959 221
  Book: same
 SHAMBLEAU Galaxy Novel 1958 127
  Book: same
Moore, C. L. and Kuttner, Henry
 EARTH'S LAST CITADEL Ace 1964 128
Moore, Ward
 BRING THE JUBILEE Ballantine 1953 196
  Book: same
 GREENER THAN YOU THINK Ballantine 1961 185
  Book: same Abr.
Moore, Ward and Davidson, Avram
 JOYLEG Pyramid 1962 160
Morley, Christopher
 THUNDER ON THE LEFT Penguin 1946 184
  Book: same
Moxley, F. Wright
 RED SNOW Simon & Schuster 1930 409
Moudy, Walter
 NO MAN ON EARTH Berkley 1964 176
Mullen, Stanley
 THE SPHINX CHILD New Collectors 1948 23
Muller, John E.
 ALIEN Badger nd 158
 BEYOND THE VOID Badger 1965 158
 BEYOND TIME Badger nd 158
 CRIMSON PLANET Badger nd 158
 DARK CONTINUUM Badger nd 158
 DAY OF THE BEASTS Badger nd 158
 THE DAY THE WORLD DIED Badger nd 158
 EDGE OF ETERNITY Badger nd 158
 THE EXORCISTS Badger nd 158
 THE EYE OF KARNAK Badger nd 158
 FORBIDDEN PLANET Badger nd 158
 IN THE BEGINNING Badger nd 158
 INFINITY MACHINE Badger nd 158
 THE MAN FROM BEYOND Badger 1965 158
 THE MAN WHO CONQUERED TIME Badger nd 158
 MARK OF THE BEAST Badger nd 158
 MICRO INFINITY Badger nd 158
 THE MIND MAKERS Badger nd 158
 THE NEGATIVE ONES Badger nd 158
 NIGHT OF THE BIG FIRE Badger nd 158
 ORBIT ONE Badger nd 158
 PERILOUS GALAXY Badger nd 158

Muller, John (Cont.)
   REACTOR XK9   Badger   nd   158
   THE RETURN OF ZEUS   Badger   nd   158
   SEARCH THE DARK STARS   Badger   nd   158
   SPACE VOID   Badger   nd   158
   SPECIAL MISSION   Badger   nd   158
   SPECTRE OF DARKNESS   1965   158
   A 1000 YEARS ON   Badger   nd   158
   THE ULTIMATE MAN   Badger   nd   158
   THE UNINVITED   Badger   nd   158
   THE UNPOSESSED   Badger   nd   158
   URANIUM 235   Badger   nd   158
   VENGEANCE OF SIVA   Badger   nd   158
   THE VENUS VENTURE   Badger   nd   158
   THE X MACHINE   Badger   nd   158
Mundy, Talbot
   FULL MOON   Royal Books   1953   225
      Book: same   with HIGH PRIEST OF CALIFORNIA which is not fantasy
   OM; THE SECRET OF AHBOR VALLEY   Xanadu (Crown)   nd   392
      Book: same
Munro, H. H.
   A SAKI SAMPLER   Military Service Pub Co   Harrisburg, Pa.   1945   155
      Book: part of THE SAKI SAMPLER
Murdock, Temple
   VULL THE INVISIBLE   Boys' Friend Library   1936   89

Nobel, Phil
   TALES FROM GEHENNA   Badger   nd   158
Noel, Sterling
   I KILLED STALIN   Eton Books   1952   190
      Book: same
   WE WHO SURVIVED   Avon   1960   160
Norris, Frank
   VANDOVER AND THE BRUTE   Grobe Press   1959   354
      Book: same
North, Andrew
   *PLAGUE SHIP   Ace   1959   178
      with VOODOO PLANET   Ace   1959   78
      *Book: PLAGUE SHIP
   SARGASSO OF SPACE   Ace   1957   192
      Book: same   with Dick THE COSMIC PUPPETS
Norton, Andre
   CATSEYE   Ace   1962   176
      Book: same
   THE DEFIANT AGENTS   Ace   1962   192
      Book: same
   GALACTIC DERELICT   Ace   1961   191
      Book: same
   JUDGMENT ON JANUS   Ace   1964   190
      Book: same
   KEY OUT OF TIME   Ace   1964   189
      Book: same
   LORD OF THUNDER   Ace   1964   174
      Book: same

Norton, Andre (Cont.)
 ORDEAL IN OTHERWHERE Ace 1965 191
  Book: same
 *SEA SIEGE Ace 1962 176
  with EYE OF THE MONSTER Ace 1962 80
  *Book: SEA SIEGE
 STAR GATE Ace 1963 190
  Book: same
 STAR HUNTER Ace 1961 96
  *with THE BEAST MASTER Ace 1961 159
  *Book: THE BEAST MASTER Abr.
 STORM OVER WARLOCK Ace 1961 192
  Book: same
 THREE AGAINST THE WITCH WORLD Ace 1965 189
 THE TIME TRADERS Ace 1960 191
  Book: same
 WEB OF THE WITCH WORLD Ace 1964 192
 WITCH WORLD Ace 1963 222
 THE CROSSROADS OF TIME Ace 1956 169
  with Dickson MANKIND ON THE RUN
 *DAYBREAK: 2250 A. D. Ace 1954 156
  *Book: STARMAN'S SON with Padget BEYOND EARTH'S GATES
 *THE LAST PLANET Ace 1955 132
  *Book: STAR RANGERS with Nourse A MAN OBSESSED
 SECRET OF THE LOST RACE Ace 1959 132
  with Sohl ONE AGAINST HERCULUM
 THE SIOUX SPACEMAN Ace 1960 133
  with Wilson AND THEN THE TOWN TOOK OFF
 *STAR BORN Ace 1958 186
  *Book: STAR BORN with Piper A PLANET FOR TEXANS
 *STAR GUARD Ace 1957 214
  *Book: STAR GUARD with Anderson PLANET OF NO RETURN
 *THE STARS ARE OURS Ace 1955 183
  *Book: THE STARS ARE OURS with Merwin THREE FACES OF TIME
Norwood, Victor
 THE CAVES OF DEATH Scion, Ltd 1951 112
 CRY OF THE BEAST Scion, Ltd 1953 128
 THE ISLAND OF CREEPING DEATH Scion, Ltd 1952 112
 NIGHT OF THE BLACK HORROR Badger nd 158
 THE SKULL OF KANAIMA Scion, Ltd 1951 112
 THE TEMPLE OF THE DEAD Scion, Ltd 1951 112
 THE UNTAMED Scion, Ltd 1951 112
Nourse, Alan E.
 RAIDERS FROM THE RINGS Pyramid 1963 160
  Book: same
 SCAVENGERS IN SPACE Ace 1962 158
  Book: same
 TIGER BY THE TAIL Macfadden-Bartell 1964 144
  Book: same
Nourse, Alan E. and Meyer, J. A.
 THE INVADERS ARE COMING Ace 1959 224
Nourse, Alan E.
 A MAN OBSESSED Ace 1955 148
  with Norton THE LAST PLANET

Nourse, Alan E. (Eont.)
    *ROCKET TO LIMBO   Ace   1960   162
       *Book: ROCKET TO LIMBO   with Brunner ECHO IN THE SKULL
Nowlan, Philip Francis
    ARMAGEDDON: 2419 A. D.   Ace   1963   190
       Book: same

O'Donnell, Elliott
    CARAVAN OF CRIME   Grafton Pubn   Dublin   nd   64
    DREAD OF NIGHT   Pillar   Dublin   nd   32
    HELL SHIPS OF MANY WATERS   Grafton Pubn   Dublin   nd   64
Ohnet, Georges
    A WEIRD GIFT   Munro   1890   280
Ohta, Takashi and Sperry, Margaret
    THE GOLDEN WIND   Boni   1930   227
Oliver, Chad
    ANOTHER KIND   Ballantine   1955   170   Book: same
    SHADOWS IN THE SUN   Ballantine   1954   152
       Book: same
    UNEARTHLY NEIGHBORS   Ballantine   1960   144
    THE WINDS OF TIME   Pocket Books   1958   132
       Book: same
Orkow, Ben
    WHEN TIME STOOD STILL   Signet   1962   174
Orwell, George
    ANIMAL FARM   Signet   1956   128
       Book: same
    1984   Signet   1950   267
       Book: same
Otterbourge, Edwin M.
    ALICE IN RANKBUSTLAND   Williams   1923   84
Owen, Dean
    THE BRIDES OF DRACULA   Monarch   1960   141
    END OF THE WORLD   Ace   1962   127
    KONGA   Monarch   1960   144
    REPTILICUS   Monarch   1961   143

Padgett, Lewis
    CHESSBOARD PLANET   Galaxy Novel   1956   124
       Book: TOMORROW AND TOMORROW and THE FAIRY CHESSMEN
    LINE TO TOMORROW   Bantam   1954   184
       Book: A GNOME THERE WAS
    WELL OF THE WORLDS   Galaxy Novel   1958   126
Padgett, Lewis and Moore, C. L.
    BEYOND EARTH'S GATES   Ace   1954   144
       with Norton DAYBREAK: 2250 A. D.
Palmer, Raymond A.
    STRANGE OFFSPRING   Utopia Pubn   nd   36
Paneth, Rita Zona
    LEGENDS AND TALES   Alliance Press   London   1944   59'
Pangborn, Edgar
    DAVY   Ballantine   1964   265
       Book: same

Pangborn, Edgar (Cont.)
    A MIRROR FOR OBSERVERS   Dell   1958   223
        Book: same
Park, Jordon
    VALERIE   Lion Books   1953   158
Parker, E. Frank
    GIRL IN TROUBLE   Utopia Pubn   nd   27
Parkman, Sydney
    SHIP ASHORE   Novel Selections   nd   128
        Book: same Abr.
Paulton, Edward
    THE AMERICAN FAUST   Belford   1890   256
Pemberton, Max
    THE SHADOW ON THE SEA   Westbrook   Cleveland   nd   298
Perutz, Leo
    THE MASTER OF THE DAY OF JUDGMENT   Boni   1930   195
Petaja, Emil
    ALPHA YES, TERRA NO!   Ace   1965   156
        with Delany THE BALLAD OF BETA - 2
Phillips, Alexander M.
    MEATH OF THE MOON   Malian   Sydney   nd   34
Phillips, Mark
    BRAIN TWISTER   Pyramid   1962   144
    THE IMPOSSIBLES   Pyramid   1963   157
    SUPERMIND   Pyramid   1963   192
Phillips, Rog
    TIME TRAP   Century Pubn   Chicago   1949   158
    WORLD OF IF   Century Pubn   Chicago   1951   126
    WORLDS WITHIN   Century Pubn   Chicago   1950   159
Piper, H. Beam
    THE COSMIC COMPUTER   Ace   1964   190
        Book: JUNKYARD PLANET
    LORD KALVAN OF OTHERWHEN   Ace   1965   186
    LITTLE FUZZY   Avon   1962   160
    THE OTHER HUMAN RACE   Avon   1964   190
    SPACE VIKING   Ace   1963   191
    A PLANET FOR TEXANS   Ace   1958   101
        with Norton STAR BORN
    CRISIS IN 2140   Ace   1957   120
        with Judd GUNNER CADE
Poe, Edgar Allan
    THE FALL OF THE HOUSE OF USHER   Signet   1960   383
        Book: parts of several
    GREAT TALES AND POEMS   Pocket Books   1960   432
        Book: parts of several
Poe, Edgar allan and Verne, Jules
    THE MYSTERY OF ARTHUR GORDON PYM   Associated Booksellers   Westport, Conn.
        1961   191
        Book: same (started by Poe - finished by Verne)
Poe, Edgar Allan (re-written by Sheridan, Lee)
    THE PIT AND THE PENDULUM   Lancer   1961   144
Poe, Edgar Allan (re-written by Dunne, Max Hallan)
    THE PREMATURE BURIAL   Lancer   1962   122
Poe, Edgar Allan (re-written by Sudak, Eunice)
    TALES OF TERROR   Lancer   1962   126

Pohl, Frederick
   THE ABOMINABLE EARTHMAN   Ballantine   1963   159
   ALTERNATING CURRENTS   Ballantine   1956   154
      Book: same
   THE CASE AGAINST TOMORROW   Ballantine   1957   152
   DRUNKARD'S WALK   Ballantine   1961   142
      Book: same
   THE MAN WHO ATE THE WORLD   Ballantine   1960   144
   SLAVE SHIP   Ballantine   1957   148
      Book: same
   TOMORROW TIMES SEVEN   Ballantine   1959   160
   TURN LEFT AT THURSDAY   Ballantine   1961   157
Pohl, Frederick (Editor)
   BEYOND THE END OF TIME   Permabooks   1952   407
   SHADOW OF TOMORROW   Permabooks   1953   386
   STAR OF STARS   Ballantine   1964   224
      Book: same
   STAR SCIENCE FICTION STORIES   Ballantine   1953   202
      Book: same
   STAR SCIENCE FICTION STORIES No. 2   Ballantine   1953   195
      Book: same
   STAR SCIENCE FICTION STORIES No. 3   Ballantine   1954   186
      Book: same
   STAR SCIENCE FICTION STORIES No. 4   Ballantine   1958   157
   STAR SCIENCE FICTION No. 5   Ballantine   1959   159
   STAR SCIENCE FICTION No. 6   Ballantine   1960   156
   STAR SHORT NOVELS   Ballantine   1954   168
      Book: same
Pohl, Frederick and Kornbluth, C. M.
   GLADIATOR-AT-LAW   Ballantine   1955   171
      Book: same
   SEARCH THE SKY   Ballantine   1954   165
      Book: same
   THE SPACE MERCHANTS   Ballantine   1953   158
      Book: same
   WOLFBANE   Ballantine   1959   140
   THE WONDER EFFECT   Ballantine   1962   159
Pohl, Frederick and Williamson, Jack
   THE REEFS OF SPACE   Ballantine   1964   188
Pollard, A. O.
   THE MURDER GERM   Hutchinson   London   1937   288
Pomeroy, William C.
   THE LORDS OF MISRULE   Laird & Lee   Chicago   1894   316   Ill.
Potocki, Jan
   THE SARAGOSSA MANUSCRIPT   Avon   1962   224
      Book: same
Powers, M. L.
   BLACK ABYSS   Badger   nd   158
Praed, (Mrs.) Campbell
   THE BROTHER OF THE SHADOW   Routledge   London   1886   158
Pragnell, Festus
   THE TERROR FROM TIMORKAL   Bear   London   1946   192
Pratt, Fletcher
   ALIEN PLANET   Ace   1964   188
      Book: same

Pratt, Fletcher (Cont.)
    DOUBLE JEOPARDY   Galaxy Novel   1957   128
        Book: same
    INVADERS FROM RIGEL   Airmont   1964   127
        Book: same
    THE UNDYING FIRE   Ballantine   1953   148
        Book: same
Pratt, Theodore
    ESCAPE TO EDEN   Fawcett   1953   266
Prime, Lord
    MR. JONNEMACHER'S MACHINE   Knickerbocker   Philadelphia   1898   255
Purdom, Tom
    I WANT THE STARS   Ace   1964   115
        with Bulmer DEMON'S WORLD

"Q"
    I SAW THREE SHIPS   Cassell   1892   288

Rabelais, Francois
    THE HISTORIES OF GARGANTUA AND PANTAGRUEL   Penguin   Middlesex   1955   71
        Book: same
Radcliffe, Ann
    THE MYSTERIES OF UDOLPHO   Juniper Press   nd   381
        Book: same Abr.
Radford, Guy
    THE ANDES TRAIL   Pocket Editions   London   nd   16
Rame, David
    TUNNEL FROM CALAIS   Armed Services Edition   nd   285
        Book: same
Ramsey, Milton W.
    THE AUSTRAL GLOBE   Ramsey   Minneapolis   1892   219   Ill.
Rand, Ayn
    ANTHEM   Signet   1961   156
        Book: same
    ATLAS SHRUGGED   Signet   1958   1084
        Book: same
Raspe, R. E.
    BARON MUNCHAUSEN   Dover   1960   192
        Book: same
Rayer, F. G.
    EARTH OUR NEW EDEN   Hamilton   nd   109
    THE STAR SEEKER   Pearson   London   nd   64
    WE CAST NO SHADOW   Hamilton   nd   108
    WORLDS AT WAR   Tempest   Bolton, Lancs.   nd   128
Reed, David V.
    MURDER IN SPACE   Galaxy Novel   1954   126
    THE THING THAT MADE LOVE   Universal   nd   160
    THE WHISPERING GORILLA   Pemberton   1950   160
Reed, Van
    DWELLERS IN SPACE   Warren   1953   128
        Book: same
    HOUSE OF MANY CHANGES   Warren   1952   128
Reiser, Marx
    BEFORE THE BEGINNING   Pearson   London   nd   64

Rohmer, Sax (Cont.)
 DAUGHTER OF FU MANCHU   Pyramid   1964   190
  Book: same
 THE DAY THE WORLD ENDED   Ace   1964   223
  Book: same
 THE DRUMS OF FU MANCHU   Pyramid   1962   162
  Book: same
 EMPEROR FU MANCHU   Fawcett   1959   208
  Book: same
 THE FIRE GODDESS   Fawcett   1953   156
  Book: virgin in flames
 THE GOLDEN SCORPION   Novel Selections   nd   128
  Book: same
 THE HAND OF FU MANCHU   Pyramid   1962   192
  Book: same
 HANGOVER HOUSE   Graphic Books   1950   188
  Book: same
 THE INSIDIOUS DR. FU MANCHU   Pyramid   1961   191
  Book: same
 THE ISLAND OF FU MANCHU   Pyramid   1963   208
  Book: same
 THE MASK OF FU MANCHU   Pyramid   1962   191
  Book: same
 THE MYSTERY OF DR. FU MANCHU   Penguin   1955   224
  Book: THE INSIDIOUS DR. FU MANCHU
 NUDE IN MINK   Fawcett   1951   188
  Book: SINS OF SUMURU
 PRESIDENT FU MANCHU   Pyramid   1963   223
  Book: same
 RE-ENTER FU MANCHU   Fawcett   1957   144
  Book: same
 THE RETURN OF FU MANCHU   Pyramid   1961   192
  Book: same
 THE RETURN OF SUMURU   Fawcett   1955   176
  Book: SAND AND SATIN
 SHADOW OF FU MANCHU   Pyramid   1963   159
  Book: same
 SINISTER MADONNA   Fawcett   1956   156
  Book: same
 SLAVES OF SUMURU   Fawcett   1952   156
  Book: same
 TALES OF CHINATOWN   Popular Library   1950   224
  Book: same
 THE TRAIL OF FU MANCHU   Pyramid   1964   220
  Book: same
Romans, R. H.
 THE MOON CONQUERORS   Swan   nd   176
Romilius, Arn
 BEYOND GEO   Warren   1953   159
 BRAIN PALAEO   Warren   1953   159
Ronald, Bruce W.
 OUR MAN IN SPACE   Ace   1965   131
  with Sharkey ULTIMATUM IN 2050 A. D.
Rose, Lawrence F.
 THE HELL FRUIT   Pearson   London   nd   64

Roshwald, Mordecai
 LEVEL 7   Signet   1961   143
    Book: same
Rosmanith, Olga
 UNHOLY FLAME   Fawcett   1952   184
Rosny, J. H.
 QUEST OF THE DAWN MAN   Ace   1964   156
    Book: THE GIANT CAT
Rowe, John G.
 THE AERIEL WAR: SUPREMACY OF THE SKIES   Vanguard Library   London   nd   17
Royer, Louis-Charles
 WHERE THEY BREED   Harborough   Stoke-on-Trent   1950   160
Russell, Eric Frank
 DEEP SPACE   Bantam   1955   165
    Book: same Abr.
 DREADFUL SANCTUARY   Lancer   1963   174
    Book: same Abr.
 THE GREAT EXPLOSION   Pyramid   1963   160
    Book: same
 MEN, MARTIANS AND MACHINES   Berkley   1958   174
    Book: same
 SINISTER BARRIER   Galaxy Novel   1950   126
    Book: same Abr.
 *SENTINELS OF SPACE   Ace   1954   172
    with THE ULTIMATE INVADER   Ace   1954   140
    *Book: SENTINELS FROM SPACE
 *THE SPACE WILLIES   Ace   1958   131
    with SIX WORLDS YONDER   Ace   1958   125
    *Book; NEXT OF KIN
  WASP   Pocket Books   1959   170
    Book: same
 *THREE TO CONQUER   Ace   1957   181
    *Book: same   with Williams DOOMSDAY EVE
Russell, John
 THE LOST GOD   Pocket Books   1946   309
Russell, Ray
 SARDONICUS   Ballantine   1961   143
Russell, W. Clark
 THE FROZEN PIRATE   Street & Smith   nd   250
    Book: same

Saberhagen, Fred
 THE GOLDEN PEOPLE   Ace   1964   118
    with Wright EXILE FROM XANADU
Safroni-Middleton, A.
 THE DREAMING SKULL   World Wide   London   nd   244
St. Clair, Margaret
 MESSAGE FROM THE EOCENE   Ace   1964   114
    with THREE WORLDS OF FUTURITY   Ace   1964   142
 SIGN OF THE LABRYS   Bantam   1963   139
 AGENT OF THE UNKNOWN   Ace   1956   128
    with Dick THE WORLD JONES MADE
 THE GAMES OF NEITH   Ace   1960   149
    with Bulmer THE EARTH GODS ARE COMING

St. Clair, Margaret (Cont.)
    THE GREEN QUEEN   Ace   1956   190
        with McClary 3 THOUSAND YEARS
St. Germain, Marie
    TALES OF THE WEIRD AND THE WEST COUNTREE   Brendon & Son   Plymouth, England
        1924   142
Sala, George Augustus and Others
    STORIES WITH A VENGEANCE   Dick's English Library   London   nd   134
Sandforde, S.
    THE THOUGHT READER   Barton   London   nd   32
Sarban
    THE DOLL MAKER   Ballantine   1960   144
        Book: same
    RINGSTONES   Ballantine   1961   139
        Book: same
    THE SOUND OF HIS HORN   Ballantine   1960   125
        Book: same
Sayers, Dorothy L. (Editor)
    HUMAN AND INHUMAN STORIES   Macfadden-Bartell   1963   176
        Book: part of THE OMNIBUS OF CRIME
    STORIES OF THE SUPERNATURAL   Macfadden-Bartell   1963   144
        Book: part of THE OMNIBUS OF CRIME
    TALES OF DETECTION AND MYSTERY   Macfadden-Bartell   1962   159
        Book: part of THE OMNIBUS OF CRIME
Sazanami, Iwaya
    BUN-BUKU CHAGAMA   Hokussido Press   Tokyo   1938   21
    KACHI-KACHI   Hokussido Press   Tokyo   1938   24
    MONOGUSA TARO   Hokussido Press   Tokyo   1938   24
    TAMA-MO-I   Hokussido Press   Tokyo   1938   38
    TAWARE TODA HIDESATO   Hokussido Press   Tokyo   1938   24
Schmitz, James H.
    AGENT OF VEGA   Pocket Books   1962   185
        Book: same
    THE UNIVERSE AGAINST HER   Ace   1964   160
Schneider, John G.
    THE GOLDEN KAZOO   Dell   1956   224
        Book: same
Science Fiction Classics
    #1 Coleridge, John
        MARTIAN MARTYRS   Columbia Pub   nd   24
    #2 Clive, Dennis
        VALLEY OF PRETENDERS   Columbia Pub   nd   24
    #3 Callahan, William
        THE MACHINE THAT THOUGHT   Columbia Pub   nd   24
    #4 Coleridge, John
        THE NEW LIFE   Columbia Pub   nd   24
    #5 Clive, Dennis
        THE VOICE COMMANDS   Columbia Pub   nd   24
    #6 Olsen, Bob
        RYTHM RIDES THE ROCKET   Columbia Pub   nd   24
Science Fiction Series
    #1 Williamson, Jack and Breuer, Miles J.
        THE GIRL FROM MARS   Stellar Pub   1930   28

Science Fiction Series (Cont.)
    #2 Keller, David H.
       THE THOUGHT PROJECTOR   Stellar Pub   1930   28
    #3 Michelmore, R.
       AN ADVENTURE IN VENUS   Stellar Pub   1930   28
    #4 Stone, Leslie
       WHEN THE SUN WENT OUT   Stellar Pub   1930   28
    #5 Lorraine, Lilith
       THE BRAIN OF THE PLANET   Stellar Pub   1930   28
    #6 Colladay, Charles H.
       WHEN THE MOON FELL   Stellar Pub   1930   28
    #7 Long, Amelia Reynolds
       THE MECHANICAL MAN
          with Bourne, Frank
          THE THOUGHT STEALER   Stellar Pub   1930   28
    #8 Bradley, Jack
       THE TORCH OF RA   Stellar Pub   1930   28
    #9 Eberle, Merab
       THE THOUGHT TRANSLATOR
          with Mitchell, M. Milton
          THE CREATION   Stellar Pub Co   1930   28
    #10 Higginson, H. W.
        THE ELIXIR   Stellar Pub   1930   28
    #11 Black, Pansey E.
        THE VALLEY OF THE GREAT RAY   Stellar Pub   1930   28
    #12 Farrar, Clyde
        THE LIFE VAPOR
           with Sharp, D. D.
           THIRTY MILES DOWN   Stellar Pub   1930   28
    #13 Black, Pansy E.
        THE MEN FROM THE METEOR   Stellar Pub   1932   24
    #14 Renard, Maurice
        THE FLIGHT OF THE AEROFIX   Stellar Pub   1932   24
    #15 Wellman, Manly Wade
        THE INVADING ASTEROID   Stellar Pub   1932   24
    #16 Smith, Clark Ashton
        IMMORTALS OF MERCURY   Stellar Pub   1932   24
    #17 Mack, Thomas
        THE SPECTRE BULLET
           with Sprissler, Alfred
           THE AVENGING NOTE   Stellar Pub   1932   24
    #18 Parzer, Sidney
        THE SHIP FROM NOWHERE   Stellar Pub   1932   24
Scott, Warwick
    DOOMSDAY   Lion Books   1953   158
       Book: same
Scott-Moncrief, D.
    NOT FOR THE SQUEAMISH   Background Books   London   1948   108
Senmark
    THE AVENGING RAY   Hodder & Stoughton   London   1952   191
       Book: same   (by Small, Austin J.)
Searel, George
    THE FALL.   A TALE OF EDEN   Lessing   Pittsburgh   1918   62
Sellings, Arthur
    TELEPATH   Ballantine   1962   160

Serling, Rod (Editor)
MORE STORIES FROM THE TWILIGHT ZONE   Bantam   1961   149
NEW STORIES FROM THE TWILIGHT ZONE   Bantam   1962   122
STORIES FROM THE TWILIGHT ZONE   Bantam   1960   151
WITCHES, WARLOCKS AND WEREWOLVES   Bantam   1963   181
Sharkey, Jack
THE SECRET MARTIANS   Ace   1961   132
   with Brunner SANCTUARY IN THE SKY
UNTIMATUM IN 2050 A. D.   Ace   1965   120
   with Ronald CUR MAN IN SPACE
Sharp, Margery
THE STONE OF CHASTITY   Avon   1949   147
   Book: same
Shaw, Brian
"ARGENTIS"   Warren   1952   112
LOST WORLD   Warren   1953   128
   Book: same
SHIPS OF VERO   Warren   1952   128
Z FORMATION   Warren   1953   159
Shaw, David
LABORATORY "X"   Warren   nd   128
PLANET FEDERATION   Warren   nd   128
SPACE MEN   Warren   nd   128
Shaw, Larry T. (Editor)
GREAT SCIENCE FICTION ADVENTURES   Lancer   1963   174
Shearing, Joseph
THE SPECTRAL BRIDE   Berkley   1965   150
   Book: THE FETCH
Sheckley, Robert
CITIZEN IN SPACE   Ballantine   1955   200
IMMORTALITY, INC.   Bantam   1959   152
   Book: IMMORTALITY DELIVERED
NOTIONS: UNLIMITED   Bantam   1960   190
PILGRIMAGE TO EARTH   Bantam   1957   167
SHARDS OF SPACE   Bantam   1962   152
THE STATUS CIVILIZATION   Signet   1960   127
STORE OF INFINITY   Bantam   1960   151
UNTOUCHED BY HUMAN HANDS   Ballantine   1954   169
   Book: same
Sheldon, Roy
ATOMS IN ACTION   Panther   1954   159
   Book: same
HOUSE OF ENTROPY   Panther   1954   159
   Book: same
MAMMOTH MAN   Hamilton   1951   128
THE MENACING SLEEP   Hamilton   1952   128
THE METAL EATER   Hamilton   1954   159
MOMENT OUT OF TIME   Hamilton   1951   110
TWO DAYS OF TERROR   Hamilton   1952   112
Shelley, Mary W.
FRANKENSTEIN   Airmont   1963   191
   Book: same
Sherman, Harold M.
THE GREEN MAN   Century Pubn   Chicago   1946   128

Shiel, M. P.
  DR. KRASINSKI'S SECRET   Book League   1929   236
    Book: same
  HOW THE OLD WOMAN GOT HOME   Collier   1961   318
    Book: same
  LORD OF THE SEA   Xanadu (Crown)   nd   299
    Book: same
Shiras, Wilmar H.
  CHILDREN OF THE ATOM   Avon   1955   192
    Book: same
Shute, Nevil
  IN THE WET   Pocket Books   1958   280
    Book: same
  AN OLD CAPTIVITY   Lancer   1962   224
    Book: same
  ON THE BEACH   Signet   1958   238
    Book: same
Silverberg, Robert
  GODLING, GO HOME   Belmont   1964   157
  NEXT STOP THE STARS   Ace   1962   114
    with THE SEED OF EARTH   Ace   1962   139
  RECALLED TO LIFE   Lancer   1962   144
  REGAN'S PLANET   Pyramid   1964   141
  *COLLISION COURSE   Ace   1961   135
    *Book: same   with Brackett THE NEMESIS FROM TERRA
  INVADERS FROM EARTH   Ace   1958   169
    with Grinnell ACROSS TIME
  MASTER OF LIFE AND DEATH   Ace   1957   128
    with White THE SECRET VISITORS
  THE PLANET KILLERS   Ace   1959   131
    with Anderson WE CLAIM THESE STARS
  THE SILENT INVADERS   Ace   1963   117
    with Temple BATTLE ON VENUS
  STEPSONS OF TERRA   Ace   1958   128
    with Wright A MAN CALLED DESTINY
  THE 13th IMMORTAL   Ace   1957   129
    with Gunn THIS FORTRESS WORLD
Simak, Clifford D.
  ALL THE TRAPS OF EARTH AND OTHER STORIES   Macfadden-Bartell   1963   158
    Book: same
  CITY   Permabooks   1954   192
    Book: same
  THE CREATOR   Crawford Pubs   Los Angeles   1946   48
  EMPIRE   Galaxy Novel   1951   160
  FIRST HE DIED   Dell   1952   222
    Book: TIME AND AGAIN
  OTHER WORLDS OF CLIFFORD SIMAK   Avon   1962   143
    Book: part of THE WORLDS OF CLIFFORD SIMAK
  STRANGERS IN THE UNIVERSE   Berkley   1957   191
    Book: same
  THEY WALKED LIKE MEN   Macfadden-Bartell   1963   176
    Book: same
  TIME AND AGAIN   Ace   1963   256
    Book: same

Simak, Clifford D. (Cont.)
  TIME IS THE SIMPLEST THING   Fawcett   1962   192
    Book: same
  WAY STATION   Macfadden-Bartell   1965   148
    Book: same
  THE WORLDS OF CLIFFORD SIMAK   Avon   1962   191
    Book: part of THE WORLDS OF CLIFFORD SIMAK
  WORLDS WITHOUT END   Belmont   1964   140
 *RING AROUND THE SUN   Ace   1954   147
   *Book: same   with de Camp COSMIC MANHUNT
  TROUBLE WITH TYCHO   Ace   1961   82
    with Chandler BRING BACK YESTERDAY
Simpson, D. G. B.
  ANTI-GAS   Barton   London   nd   32
Siodmak, Curt
  DONOVAN'S BRAIN   Bantam   1950   181
    Book: same
  RIDERS TO THE STARS   Ballantine   1953   166
  SKYPORT   Signet   1961   159
    Book: same
Sissons, Michael (Editor)
  IN THE DEAD OF NIGHT   Panther   1962   182
    Book: same
Slaughter, Frank G.
  EPEDEMIC   Pocket Books   1962   277
    Book: same
Slee, Richard and Pratt, Cornelia Atwood
  DR. BERKELEY'S DISCOVERY   Putnam   1899   219
Sloane, William
  THE UNQUIET CORPSE   Dell   1956   224
    Book: THE EDGE OF RUNNING WATER
  TO WALK THE NIGHT   Dell   1955   223
    Book: same
Smith, Clark Ashton
  THE DOUBLE SHADOW AND OTHER FANTASIES   Auburn Journal   Auburn, Calif.
    1933   36
  THE WHITE SIBYL   Fantasy Pub   Everett, Pa.   nd
    with Keller MEN OF AVAOLN   38 total pages
Smith, Cordwainer
  THE PLANET BUYER   Pyramid   1964   156
  SPACE LORDS   Pyramid   1965   170
Smith, Edward Elmer
  FIRST LENSMAN   Pyramid   1964   352
    Book: same
  GALACTIC PATROL   Fantasy Press   Reading, Pa.   1950   273
    Book: same
  THE GALAXY PRIMES   Ace   1965   192
  THE SKYLARK OF SPACE   Pyramid   1958   159
    Book: same
  THE SKYLARK OF VALERON   Pyramid   1963   206
    Book: same
  SKYLARK THREE   Pyramid   1963   207
    Book: same
Smith, Evelyn E.
  THE PERFECT PLANET   Lancer   1963   144
    Book: same

Smith, Garret
  BETWEEN WORLDS   Stellar Pub   nd   93
Smith, George O.
    THE FOURTH "R"   Ballantine   1959   160
    HELLFLOWER   Pyramid   1957   160
      Book: same
    OPERATION INTERSTELLAR   Century Pubn   Chicago   1950   127
    SPACE PLAGUE   Avon   1958   141
      Book: HIGHWAYS IN HIDING
    TROUBLED STAR   Beacon (Galaxy Novel)   1959   159
      Book: same
  *FIRE IN THE HEAVENS   Ace   1959   159
    *Book: same   with Knight MASTERS OF EVOLUTION
Smith, Thorne
    THE BISHOP'S JAEGERS   Pocket Books   1946   248
      Book: same
    DID SHE FALL?   Paperback Library   1962   223
      Book: same
    THE GLORIOUS POOL   Pocket Books   1946   240
      Book: same
    THE NIGHT LIFE OF THE GODS   Pyramid   1961   256
      Book: same
    SKIN AND BONES   Pocket Books   1948   274
      Book: same
    THE STRAY LAMB   Avon   1945   162
      Book: same
    TOPPER   Pocket Books   1939   236
      Book: same
    TOPPER TAKES A TRIP   Pyramid   1962   256
      Book: same
    TURNABOUT   Pocket Books   1947   277
      Book: same
Sohl, Jerry
    THE ALTERED EGO   Pennant Books   1955   120
      Book: same
    COSTIGAN'S NEEDLE   Bantam   1954   169
      Book: same
    THE HAPLOIDS   Lion Books   1953   191
      Book: same
    POINT ULTIMATE   Bantam   1959   151
      Book: same
    THE TIME DISSOLVER   Avon   1957   158
    THE TRANSCENDENT MAN   Bantam   1959   154
      Book: same
    THE MARS MONOPOLY   Ace   1956   183
      with Miller THE MAN WHO LIVED FOREVER
    ONE AGAINST HERCULUM   Ace   1959   124
      with Norton SECRET OF THE LOST RACE
Southern, Terry
    THE MAGIC CHRISTIAN   Berkley   1961   137
      Book: same
Southworth, (Mrs.) E D E N
    THE HAUNTED HOMESTEAD AND OTHER NOVELETTES   Street & Smith   1901   236
    THE TRAIL OF THE SERPENT   Street & Smith   1879   226

Spector, Robert Donald (Editor)
   SEVEN MASTERPIECES OF GOTHIC HORROR   Bantam   1963   465
Speight, T. W.
   AS IT WAS WRITTEN   Chatto & Windus   London   1901   132
Stables, Gordon
   FROM POLE TO POLE   Street & Smith   1901   345
     Book: same
   WILD ADVENTURES ROUND THE POLE   Street & Smith   1904   318
     Book: same
Stamper, W. J.
   BEYOND THE SEAS   No publisher   Norfolk, Va.   1935   215
Stanton, Paul
   VILLAGE OF STARS   Pocket Books   1962   213
     Book: same
Stapledon, Olaf
   LAST AND FIRST MEN   Penguin   1938   238
     Book: same
   ODD JOHN   Galaxy Novel   1951   126
     Book: same Abr.
   THE STAR MAKER   Berkley   1961   222
     Book: same
Statten, Vargo
   ACROSS THE AGES   Scion, Ltd   1952   96
   ANNIHILATION!   Scion, Ltd   nd   128
   THE AVENGING MARTIAN   Scion, Ltd   1951   128
   THE BLACK AVENGER   Scion, Ltd   1953   128
   BLACK BARGAIN   Scion, Ltd   1953   128
   BLACK WING OF MARS   Scion, Ltd   1953   128
   BORN OF LUNA   Scion, Ltd   1951   128
   CATACLYSM   Scion, Ltd   1951   128
   THE CATALYST   Scion, Ltd   1951   112
   THE COSMIC FLAME   Scion, Ltd   1950   128
   DEADLINE TO PLUTO   Scion, Ltd   1951   128
   DECREATION   Scion, Ltd   1952   96
   THE DEVOURING FIRE   Scion, Ltd   1951   112
   THE DUST DESTROYERS   Scion, Ltd   1953   127
   THE ECLIPSE EXPRESS   Scion, Ltd   1952   112
   THE G-BOMB   Scion, Ltd   1952   112
   THE GRAND ILLUSION   Scion, Ltd   1954   128
   INFERNO   Scion, Ltd   1950   128
   INNER COSMOS   Scion, Ltd   1952   112
   THE INTERLOPER   Scion, Ltd   1953   128
   THE LAST MARTIAN   Scion, Ltd   1952   96
   LAUGHTER IN SPACE   Scion, Ltd   1952   112
   THE LIE DETECTOR   Scion, Ltd   1953   127
   MAN IN DUPLICATE   Scion, Ltd   1953   128
   THE MAN FROM TOMORROW   Scion, Ltd   1952   112
   MAN OF TWO WORLDS   Scion, Ltd   1953   128
   THE MICRO MEN   Scion, Ltd   1950   128
   THE MULTIMAN   Scion, Ltd   1954   128
   NEBULA X   Scion, Ltd   1950   128
   THE NEW SATELLITE   Scion, Ltd   1951   112
   ODYSSEY OF NINE   Scion, Ltd   1953   128
   1000 YEAR VOYAGE   Scion, Ltd   1954   128

Sturgeon, Theodore (Cont.)
   CAVIAR   Ballantine   1955   157
      Book: same
   THE COSMIC RAPE   Dell   1958   160
   E PLURIBUS UNICORN   Ballantine   1956   212
      Book: same
   MORE THAN HUMAN   Ballantine   1953   188
      Book: same
   NOT WITHOUT SORCERY   Ballantine   1961   160
      Book: same
   SOME OF YOUR BLOOD   Ballantine   1960   188
   STURGEON IN ORBIT   Pyramid   1964   159
   THE SYNTHETIC MAN   Pyramid   1958   174
      Book: THE DREAMING JEWELS
   A TOUCH OF STRANGE   Berkley   1959   174
      Book: same
   VENUS PLUS X   Pyramid   1960   160
   VOYAGE TO THE BOTTOM OF THE SEA   Pyramid   1961   159
   A WAY HOME   Pyramid   1956   192
      Book: same
Sturgeon, Theodore and Simak, Clifford D. and Leinster, Murray
   THREE IN ONE   Pyramid   1963   144
Sudak, Eunice
   X   Lancer   1963   126
Sutton, Jeff
   APOLLO AT GO   Popular Library   1964   159
   BOMBS IN ORBIT   Ace   1959   192
   FIRST ON THE MOON   Ace   1958   192
   SPACEHIVE   Ace   1960   192
Swain, Dwight V.
   THE TRANSPOSED MAN   Ace   1955   95
      with McIntosh ONE IN THREE HUNDRED
Swift, Jonathan
   GULLIVER'S TRAVELS   Signet   1960   319
      Book: same

Tabori, Paul
   THE GREEN RAIN   Pyramid   1961   192
Taine, John
   THE GREATEST ADVENTURE   Ace   1958   256
      Book: same
   SEEDS OF LIFE   Galaxy Novel   1953   126
      Book: same Abr.
   THE TIME STREAM
      with THE GREATEST ADVENTURE
      with THE PURPLE SAPPHIRE   Dover   1964   532
      Books: same Abr.
Talbot, Daniel (Editor)
   THE DAMNED   Lion Library   1954   191
Taylor, Robert Lewis
   ADRIFT IN A BONEYARD   Avon   1963   191
      Book: same
Teilhet, Darwin L.
   THE FEAR MAKERS   Pocket Books   1946   218
      Book: same

Temple, William F.
 THE FOUR SIDED TRIANGLE Galaxy Novel 1952 126
  Book: same Abr.
 THE AUTOMATED GOLIATH Ace 1962 143
  with THE THREE SUNS OF AMARA Ace 1962 80
 BATTLE ON VENUS Ace 1963 104
  with Silverberg THE SILENT INVADERS
Tenn, William
 THE HUMAN ANGLE Ballantine 1956 152
  Book: same
 OF ALL POSSIBLE WORLDS Ballantine 1955 159
  Book: same
 TIME IN ADVANCE Bantam 1958 153
Tenn, William (Editor)
 OUTSIDERS: CHILDREN OF WONDER Permabooks (Doubleday) 1954 355
  Book: CHILDREN OF WONDER
Tevis, Walter
 THE MAN WHO FELL TO EARTH Fawcett 1963 144
Thanet, Neil
 BEYOND THE VEIL Badger nd 158
 THE MAN WHO CAME BACK Badger nd 158
Thayer, Tiffany
 ONE MAN SHOW Avon 1951 251
  Book: same
Thomas, Chauncey
 THE CRYSTAL BUTTON; OR, ADVENTURES OF PAUL PROGNOSIS IN THE FORTY-NINTH CENTURY
  Fenno 1889 302
  Book: same
Thomson, Christine Campbell (Editor)
 MORE NOT AT NIGHT Arrow Books 1961 192
  Book: same
 NOT AT NIGHT Arrow Books 1960 192
  Book: same
 STILL NOT AT NIGHT Arrow Books 1962 192
  Book: same
Thorpe, D. N.
 FIVE FACES OF FEAR Badger nd 158
 LIGHTNING WORLD Badger nd 158
Thorpe, Fred
 THE BOY IN BLACK; OR, STRANGE ADVENTURES AMONG STRANGE PEOPLE
  Street & Smith 1903 208
 THE SILENT CITY; OR, QUEER ADVENTURES AMONG QUEER PEOPLE Street & Smith
  1907 314
Titan, Erle
 THE GOLD OF AKADA Scion, Ltd 1951 128
Titterton, W. R.
 DEATH RAY DICTATOR AND OTHER STORIES Douglas Organ London nd 127
Tolkien, J. R. R.
 THE FELLOWSHIP OF THE RING Ace 1965 448
  Book: same
 THE HOBBIT Puffin (Penguin) 1961 284
  Book: same
 THE RETURN OF THE KING Ace 1965 392
  Book: same

Tolkien, J. R. R. (Cont.)
   THE TWO TOWERS   Ace   1965   421
      Book: same
Torro, Pei
   THE FACE OF FEAR   Badger   nd   158
   FORCE 97-X   Badger   1965   158
   FORMULA 29X   Badger   nd   158
   GALAXY 666   Badger   nd   158
   THE LOST ASTRONAUT   Badger   nd   158
   LEGION OF THE LOST   Badger   nd   158
   THE PHANTOM ONES   Badger   nd   158
   THE RETURN   Badger   nd   158
   SPACE NO BARRIER   Badger   nd   158
   THE STRANGE ONES   Badger   nd   158
   THROUGH THE BARRIER   Badger   nd   158
Tubb, E. C.
   ALIEN IMPACT   Hamilton   nd   109
   ATOM-WAR ON MARS   Hamilton   1952   112
   CITY OF NO RETURN   Scion, Ltd   1954   144
   HELL PLANET   Scion, Ltd   1954   128
   JOURNEY TO MARS   Scion, Ltd   1954   144
   MOON BASE   Ace   1964   191
      Book: same
   THE MUTANTS REBEL   Hamilton   1953   164
   THE RESURRECTED MAN   Scion, Ltd.   1954   128
   THE STELLAR LEGION   Scion, Ltd   1954   144
   VENUSIAN ADVENTURE   Comyns   London   1953   128
   WORLD AT BAY   Hamilton   1954   159
   THE MECHANICAL MONARCH   Ace   1958   165
      with Fontenay TWICE UPON A TIME
   THE SPACE BORN   Ace   1956   156
      with Dick THE MAN WHO JAPED
Tucker, Wilson
   CITY IN THE SEA   Galaxy Novel   1952   126
      Book: same Abr.
   THE LONG LOUD SILENCE   Dell   1955   192
      Book: same
   THE MAN FROM TOMORROW   Bantam   1955   148
      Book: WILD TALENT
   THE TIME MASTERS   Signet   1954   128
      Book: same
   TIME X   Bantam   1955   140
      Book: THE SCIENCE FICTION SUBTREASURY
   TOMORROW PLUS X   Avon   1957   158
      Book: TIME BOMB
Tulip, J.
   THE MOON GODDESS   Halle   London   nd   64
Tucker, Wilson
   TO THE TOMBAUGH STATION   Ace   1960   145
      with Anderson EARTHMAN GO HOME
Turnerolli, Tracy
   A RUSSION PRINCESS, AND A RUSSIAN GHOST STORY   Hansom Cab   London   nd   190
Turney, Catherine
   THE OTHER ONE   Dell   1954   224
      Book: same

wain, Mark
   THE COMPLETE SHORT STORIES   Bantam   1958   679
      Book: same
   A CONNECTICUT YANKEE IN KING ARTHUR'S COURT   Pocket Books   1948   360
      Book: same
   THE MYSTERIOUS STRANGER   Signet   1962   256
      Book: same
weed, Thomas F.
   GABRIEL OVER THE WHITE HOUSE   Kemsley Newspapers   London   1951   190
      Book: same
weedale, Violet
   PHANTOMS OF THE DAWN   J. Long   London   1938   255

Valdez, Paul
   THE FATAL FOCUS   Transport Pub Co   1950   49
   GHOSTS DON'T KILL   Transport Pub Co   1950   34
   KILLER BY NIGHT   Transport Pub Co   1950   32
   THE TIME THIEF   Transport Pub Co   nd   34
Van der Elst, Violet
   DEATH OF THE VAMPIRE BARONESS   Van der Elst Press   London   1945   80
   THE MUMMY COMES TO LIFE   Van der Elst Press   London   nd   79
   THE SATANIC POWER   Van der Elst Press   London   nd   81
   THE SECRET POWER   Van der Elst Press   London   nd   80
   THE STRANGE DOCTOR   Van der Elst Press   London   nd   81
Van Loden, Erle
   CURSE OF PLANET KUZ   Self   1951   128
   VOYAGE INTO SPACE   Self   1954   100
van Thal, Herbert (Editor)
   A BOOK OF STRANGE STORIES   Pan Books   1954   188
   ORIENTAL SPLENDOR   A. Baker   London   nd   325
   THE SECOND PAN BOOK OF HORROR STORIES   Pan Books   1960   319
   TOLD IN THE DARK. A BOOK OF UNCANNY STORIES   Pan Books   1950   254
   TOLD IN THE DARK. NINE UNCANNY STORIES   Pan Books   1952   191
      Reprint of first "Told in the Dark" minus two stories
van Vogt, A. E.
   AWAY AND BEYOND   Berkley   1959   172
      Book: same Abr.
   THE BEAST   Macfadden-Bartell   1964   160
      Book: same
   DESTINATION: UNIVERSE   Signet   1953   160
      Book: same
   THE HOUSE THAT STOOD STILL   Harlequin   Toronto   1952   224
      Book: same
   THE MATING CRY   Galaxy Novel   1960   160
      Book: THE HOUSE THAT STOOD STILL Abr.
   THE MIND CAGE   Avon   1958   191
      Book: same
   MISSION TO THE STARS   Berkley   1957   157
      Book: THE MIXED MEN
   THE PAWNS OF NULL A   Ace   1956   254
   SLAN   Ballantine   1961   159
      Book: same
   TWO HUNDRED MILLION A. D.   Paperback Library
      Book: THE BOOK OF PTATH

van Vogt, A. E. (Cont.)
  THE VOYAGE OF THE SPACE BEAGLE   Macfadden-Bartell   1963   192
    Book: same
  THE WAR AGAINST THE RULL   Pocket Books   1963   223
    Book: same
  THE WIZARD OF LINN   Ace   1962   190
  *THE WORLD OF NULL A   Ace   1953   147
    with THE UNIVERSE MAKER   Ace   1953   152
    *Book: THE WORLD OF NULL A
  EARTH'S LAST FORTRESS   Ace   1960   114
    with Smith LOST IN SPACE
  *EMPIRE OF THE ATOM   Ace   1957   162
    with Long SPACE STATION #1
    *Book: EMPIRE OF THE ATOM
  *ONE AGAINST ETERNITY   Ace   1955   162
    with Leinster THE OTHER SIDE OF HERE
    *Book: THE WEAPON MAKERS
  *SIEGE OF THE UNSEEN   Ace   1960   103
    with Brunner THE WORLD SWAPPERS
    *Book: FIVE SCIENCE FICTION NOVELS as "The Chronicler" (Greenberg - editor
  THE TWISTED MEN   Ace   1964   130
    with Knox ONE OF OUR ASTEROIDS IS MISSING
  *THE WEAPON SHOPS OF ISHER   Ace   1954   166
    with Leinster GATEWAY TO ELSEWHERE
    *Book: THE WEAPON SHOPS OF ISHER
Vance, Jack
  *BIG PLANET   Ace   1958   158
    with SLAVES OF THE KLAU   Ace   1958   129
    *Book: BIG PLANET
  THE DYING EARTH   Hillman Periodicals   1950   175
  *THE FIVE GOLD BANDS   Ace   1962   122
    with THE DRAGON MASTERS   Ace   1962   102
    *Originally published as "The Space Pirate"
  FUTURE TENSE   Ballantine   1964   160
  THE HOUSES OF ISZM   Ace   1964   112
    with SON OF THE TREE   Ace   1964   111
  THE KILLING MACHINE   Berkley   1964   158
  SPACE OPERA   Pyramid   1964   168
  THE SPACE PIRATE   Toby Press   1953   128
  THE STAR KING   Berkley   1964   158
  TO LIVE FOREVER   Ballantine   1956   185
    Book: same
Vercors
  THE MURDER OF THE MISSING LINK   Pocket Books   1955   196
    Book: YOU SHALL KNOW THEM
Verne, Jules
  FROM THE EARTH TO THE MOON   Fawcett   1958   222
    Book: same Abr.
  JOURNEY TO THE CENTER OF THE EARTH   Ace   1956   256
    Book: same
  MASTER OF THE WORLD   Ace   1960   254
    Book: same
  THE MYSTERIOUS ISLAND   Pocket Books   1961   554
    Book: same
  OFF ON A COMET   Ace   1957   318
    Book: HECTOR SERVADEC; OR, OFF ON A COMET

Verne, Jules (Cont.)
    THE PURCHASE OF THE NORTH POLE   Ace   1960   159
        Book: same
    *TO THE SUN?
        with OFF ON A COMET   Dover   1960   462
        *Book: TO THE SUN?
    20,000 LEAGUES UNDER THE SEA   Bantam   1962   371
        Book: same
Vernon, Roger Lee
    THE SPACE FRONTIERS   Signet   1955   152
Vidal, Gore
    MESSIAH   Ballantine   1955   201
        Book: same
    VISIT TO A SMALL PLANET   Signet   1960   127
        Book: same (play)
Viereck, George S. and Eldridge, Paul
    SALOME, MY FIRST 2,000 YEARS OF LOVE   Ace   1954   320
        Book: SALOME, THE WANDERING JEWESS Abr.
Vincent, Harl
    MASTER OF DREAMS   Utopia Pubn   nd   36
Vivian, E. Charles
    WOMAN DOMINANT   Ward, Lock   London   1930   312
Vonnegut, Kurt, Jr.
    CANARY IN A CAT HOUSE   Fawcett   1961   160
    THE SIRENS OF TITAN   Dell   1960   319
        Book: same
    UTOPIA 14   Bantam   1956   219
Wakefield, H. Russell
    THE CLOCK STRIKES TWELVE   Ballantine   1961   159
        Book: same Abr.
Wallace, F. L.
    ADDRESS: CENTAURI   Galaxy Novel   1958   158
        Book: same
Wallace, King
    THE NEXT WAR   Martyn Pub House   Washington, D. C.   1892   130
Wallis, G. MacDonald
    LEGEND OF LOST EARTH   Ace   1963   133
        with Brackett ALPHA CENTAURI OR DIE
    LIGHT OF LILITH   Ace   1961   123
        with Knight THE SUN SABOTEURS
Walpole, Horace
    THE CASTLE OF OTRANTO   G. Munro   1886   102
        Book: same
Walpole, Hugh
    PORTRAIT OF A MAN WITH RED HAIR   Avon   1949   188
        Book: same
Walsh, J. M.
    VANGUARD TO NEPTUNE   Kemsley Newspapers   London   1952   190
Walters, Hugh
    FIRST ON THE MOON   Tempo (Grosset)   1962   192
        Book: same
Walton, Evangeline
    WITCH HOUSE   Monarch   1962   159
        Book: same

Ward, Herbert D.
    A DASH TO THE POLE. A TALE OF ADVENTURE IN THE ICE-BOUND NORTH
        Street & Smith   1901   270
        Book: same
Watkin, Lawrence Edward
    DARBY O'GILL AND THE LITTLE PEOPLE   Dell   1959   159
    ON BORROWED TIME   Pocket Books   1945   184
        Book: same
Watson, W. H.
    THE COUNT DE LATOUR   Fine Arts Pub   Washington, D. C.   1898   186
Webster, F. A. M.
    SON OF ABDAN   Readers' Library   London   nd   160
Weinbaum, Stanley G.
    THE BLACK FLAME   Harlequin   Toronto   1953   223
        Book: same
    A MARTIAN ODYSSEY   Lancer   1962   159
        Book: same
    PARASITE PLANET   Whitman Press   Sydney   1950   48
Welcome, S. Byron
    FROM EARTH'S CENTER; A POLAR GATEWAY MESSAGE   Kerr   Chicago   1894   274
Welles, Orson (Editor)
    INVASION FROM MARS   Dell   1949   192
Wellman, Manly Wade
    THE BEASTS FROM BEYOND   Pemberton   1950   158
    DEVIL'S PLANET   Pemberton   1951   128
    SOJARR OF TITAN   Crestwood   nd   120
    TWICE IN TIME   Galaxy Novel   1958   159
        Book: same
    WHO FEARS THE DEVIL?   Ballantine   1965   186
        Book: same
    *THE DARK DESTROYERS   Ace   1960   111
        with Anderson BOW DOWN TO NUL
        *Book: THE DARK DESTROYERS
Wells, Barry
    THE DAY THE EARTH CAUGHT FIRE   Ballantine   1961   145
Wells, Basil and Forth, Andrew
    GRIFFIN BOOKLET ONE--SCIENCE FANTASY SERIES   Griffin Pub Co   Los Angeles
        1949   47
Wells, H. G.
    BEST STORIES   Ballantine   1958   320
        Book: parts of several
    THE FIRST MEN IN THE MOON   Ballantine   1962   160
        Book: same
    THE FOOD OF THE GODS   Ballantine   1962   189
        Book: same
    THE INVISIBLE MAN
        with THE WAR OF THE WORLDS   Pocket Books   1962   329
        Books: same
    THE ISLAND OF DR. MOREAU   Ace   1956   192
        Book: same
    THE TIME MACHINE   Berkley   1957   141
        Book: same
    WHEN THE SLEEPER WAKES   Ace   1963   283
        Book: same

Werner, A.
  THE CAPTAIN OF THE LOCUSTS   Unwin   London   1899   296
Werper, Barton
  TARZAN AND THE ABOMINABLE SNOWMAN   Monarch   1965   125
  TARZAN AND THE CAVE CITY   Monarch   1964   126
  TARZAN AND THE SILVER GLOBE   Monarch   1964   126
  TARZAN AND THE SNAKE PEOPLE   Monarch   1964   126
  TARZAN AND THE WINGED INVADERS   Monarch   1965   126
West, Wallace
  THE BIRD OF TIME   Ace   1961   224
    Book: same
  LORDS OF ATLANTIS   Airmont   1963   128
    Book: same
  THE MEMORY BANK   Airmont   1962   127
Westall, William
  THE PHANTOM CITY   Harper   1886   158
    Book: same
Weston, G.
  HIS FIRST MILLION WOMEN   Avon   1952   220
    Book: same
Weyman, Stanley
  THE MAN IN BLACK   Cassell   London   1914   127
    Book: same
Wheatley, Dennis
  BLACK AUGUST   Arrow Books   1960   320
    Book: same
  THE DEVIL RIDES OUT   Arrow Books   1954   245
    Book: same
  THE FABULOUS VALLEY   Arrow Books   1953   286
    Book: same
  THE HAUNTING OF TOBY JUG   Arrow Books   1959   352
    Book: same
  THE KA OF GIFFORD HILLARY   Arrow Books   1961   400
    Book: same
  THE MAN WHO MISSED THE WAR   Arrow Books   1960   256
    Book: same
  THE SATANIST   Arrow Books   1963   400
    Book: same
  THE SECRET WAR   Arrow Books   1953   288
    Book: same
  SIXTY DAYS TO LIVE   Arrow Books   1960   351
    Book: same
  STRANGE CONFLICT   Arrow Books   1959   291
    Book: same
  SUCH POWER IS DANGEROUS   Arrow Books   1962   256
    Book: same
  TO THE DEVIL - A DAUGHTER   Arrow Books   1956   281
    Book: same
  THEY FOUND ATLANTIS   Arrow Books   1953   256
    Book: same
  UNCHARTED SEAS   Arrow Books   1960   288
    Book: same
White, James
  DEADLY LITTER   Ballantine   1964   175
  THE ESCAPE ORBIT   Ace   1965   188

White, James (Cont.)
  HOSPITAL STATION   Ballantine   1962   191
  STAR SURGEON   Ballantine   1963   159
  SECOND ENDING   Ace   1962   100
    with Delany THE JEWELS OF APTOR
  THE SECRET VISITORS   Ace   1957   107
    with Silverberg MASTER OF LIFE AND DEATH
White, Ted
  ANDROID AVENGER   Ace   1965   110
    with Brunner THE ALTAR OF ASCONEL
White, T. H.
  THE ONCE AND FUTURE KING   Dell   1960   637
    Book: same
Whitley, Reid
  THE MASTER OF DWARF ISLAND   Boys' Friend Library   1930   65
Wibberley, Leonard
  MOUSE ON THE MOON   Bantam   1963   124
    Book: same
  THE MOUSE THAT ROARED   Bantam   1959   152
    Book: same
Wilde, Oscar
  THE PICTURE OF DORIAN GRAY   Pyramid   1961   190
    Book: same
Willeford, Charles
  THE MACHINE IN WARD 11   Belmont   1963   141
Wilhelm, Kate
  THE MILE LONG SPACESHIP   Berkely   1963   160
Williams, Herbert (Editor)
  TERROR AT NIGHT   Avon   1947   194
Williams, Nick Boddie
  THE ATOM CURTAIN   Ace   1956   168
    with Dickson ALIEN FROM ARCTURUS
Williams, Robert Moore
  THE BLUE ATOM   Ace   1959   124
    with THE VOID BEYOND   Ace   1959   130
  THE CHAOS FIGHTERS   Ace   1955   160
  THE DAY THEY H-BOMBED LOS ANGELES   Ace   1961   128
  RED DEATH OF MARS   Malian Press   Sydney   1950   34
    with Leinster, Marray THE PLANTS
  THE SECOND ATLANTIS   Ace   1965   123
  WORLD OF THE MASTERMINDS   Ace   1960   149
    with TO THE END OF TIME   Ace   1960   108
  CONQUEST OF THE SPACE SEA   Ace   1955   168
    with Brackett THE GALACTIC BREED
  THE DARKNESS BEFORE TOMORROW   Ace   1962   118
    with Woodcott LADDER IN THE SKY
  DOOMSDAY EVE   Ace   1957   138
    with Russell THREE TO CONQUER
  FLIGHT FROM YESTERDAY   Ace   1963   120
    with Laumer ENVOY TO NEW WORLDS
  KING OF THE FOURTH PLANET   Ace   1962   128
    with DeVet & MacLean COSMIC CHECKMATE
  THE LUNAR EYE   Ace   1964   115
    with Delany THE TOWERS OF TORON

Wollheim Donald A. (Editor) (Cont.)
    THE HIDDEN PLANET   Ace   1959   190
    THE MACABRE READER   Ace   1959   222
    MORE ADVENTURES ON OTHER PLANETS   Ace   1963   190
    MORE MACABRE   Ace   1961   192
    THE POCKETBOOK OF SCIENCE FICTION   Pocket Books   1943   310
    SWORDSMEN IN THE SKY   Ace   1964   192
    TALES OF OUTER SPACE   Ace   1954   160
        with ADVENTURES IN THE FAR FUTURE   Ace   1954   138
Wollheim, Donald A. and Carr, Terry (Editors)
    WORLD'S BEST SCIENCE FICTION: 1965   Ace   1965   288
Wollheim Donald A. (Editor)
    MEN ON THE MOON   Ace   1958   137
        with Leinster CITY ON THE MOON
Woodcott, Keith
    I SPEAK FOR EARTH   Ace   1961   120
        with Cummings WANDL, THE INVADER
    LADDER IN THE SKY   Ace   1962   137
        with Williams THE DARKNESS BEFORE TOMORROW
    THE MARTIAN SPHINX   Ace   1965   149
    THE PSIONIC MENACE   Ace   1963   108
        with Delany CAPTIVES OF THE FLAME
Woolrich, Cornell
    BEYOND THE NIGHT   Avon   1959   160
    THE DOOMSTONE   Avon   1960   159
Wormser, Richard
    PAN SATYRUS   Avon   1963   144
Worts, George F.
    THE MONSTER OF THE LAGOON   Popular Pubn   Toronto   1947   96
Wright, Austin Tappan
    ISLANDIA   Farrar & Rinehart   1956   1013
        Book: same
Wright, Lan
    EXILE FROM XANADU   Ace   1964   137
        with Saberhagen THE GOLDEN PEOPLE
    A MAN CALLED DESTINY   Ace   1958   128
        with Silverberg STEPSONS OF TERRA
    WHO SPEAKS OF CONQUEST   Ace   1957   160
        with Wollheim THE EARTH IN PERIL
Wright, Lee
    THE POCKET BOOK OF MYSTERY STORIES   Pocket Books   1941   439
Wright, S. Fowler
    THE AMPHIBIANS   Galaxy Novel   1951   126
        Book: same Abr.   (reprinted as first part of THE WORLD BELOW)
    THE DELUGE   Cherry Tree   London   nd   156
        Book: same
    THE ISLAND OF CAPTAIN SPARROW   Withy Grove Press   London   nd   255
        Book: same
    TWO FAMOUS STORIES: "JUSTICE" AND " THE RAT"   Books of Today   London   nd   ?
    THE WORLD BELOW   Galaxy Novel   1951   126
        Book: same Abr.   (reprinted as second part of THE WORLD BELOW)
Wu Cheng-En
    MONKEY   Grove Press   1958   305
        Book: same

Wylie, Philip
THE DISAPPEARANCE   Pocket Books   1952   384
  Book: same
GLADIATOR   Avon   1949   187
  Book: same Abr.
THE SMUGGLED ATOM BOMB   Avon   1952   126
  Book: same
TOMORROW   Popular Library   1961   288
  Book: same
Wyndham, John
THE DAY OF THE TRIFFIDS   Fawcett   1962   191
  Book: same
THE INFINITE MOMENT   Ballantine   1961   159
THE KRAKEN WAKES   Penguin   1953   182
  Book: OUT OF THE DEEPS
THE MIDWICH CUCKOOS   Ballantine   1958   247
  Book: same
OUT OF THE DEEPS   Ballantine   1953   182
  Book: same
RE-BIRTH   Ballantine   1955   185
  Book: same
REVOLT OF THE TRIFFIDS   Popular Library   1952   224
  Book: THE DAY OF THE TRIFFIDS
THE SEEDS OF TIME   Penguin   1958   204
  Book: same
TALES OF GOOSEFLESH AND LAUGHTER   Ballantine   1956   150
TROUBLE WITH LICHEN   Ballantine   1960   160
  Book: same
VILLAGE OF THE DAMNED   Ballantine   1957   189
  Book: THE MIDWICH CUCKOOS
Wyndham, John and Parkes, Lucas
THE OUTWARD URGE   Ballantine   1959   143

Yorke, Jacqueline
BRIDES OF THE DEVIL   Dennis Yates   London   nd   160
Yorke, Preston
GAMMA RAY MURDERS   Everybody's Books   nd   128

Zamiatin, Eugene
WE   Everyman   1960   196
  Book: same
Zacherley
ZACHERLEY'S MIDNIGHT SNACKS   Ballantine   1960   157
ZACHERLEY'S VULTURE STEW   Ballantine   1960   160
Zeigfried, Karl
ANDROID   Badger   nd   158
ATOMIC NEMESIS   Badger   nd   158
BARRIER 346   Badger   1965   158
BEYOND THE GALAXY   Spencer   nd   112
CHAOS IN ARCTURUS   Spencer   1953   124
CHARIOT INTO TIME   Spencer   1953   128
DARK CENTAURI   Spencer   1954   130
ESCAPE TO INFINITY   Badger   nd   158
GODS OF DARKNESS   Badger   nd   158

Zeigfried, Karl
    NO WAY BACK   Badger   nd   158
    PROJECTION INFINITY   Badger   nd   158
    RADAR ALERT   Badger   nd   158
    THE URANIUM SEEKERS   Spencer   1953   128
    WALK THROUGH TOMORROW   Badger   nd   158
    WORLD OF TOMORROW   Badger   nd   158
    THE WORLD THAT NEVER WAS   Badger   nd   158
    ZERO MINUS X   Badger   nd   158

Most of the following titles were supplied by Mr. Thomas Moriarty - thank you,

Aimard, Gustave
    THE INDIAN SCOUT   G. Munro   1891   128
        Book: same
    THE LAST OF THE AUCAS   Lovell   1887   125
        Book: same
Ainsworth, W. Harrison
    ROOKWOOD, A ROMANCE   J. Dick's English Novels   London   nd   151
        Book: same
    WINDSOR CASTLE   Dick's English Novels   London   nd   152   Ill.
        Book: same
Aldiss, Brian
    STARSWARM   Signet   1964   159
Allen, Grant
    THE DESIRE OF THE EYES AND OTHER STORIES   Fenno   1896   320
Anonymous
    HORROR STORIES   Paul Elek   London   1961   255
    IRISH FAIRY TALES AND STORIES   Haldeman-Julius   Girard, Kansas   nd   61
    TALES OF TERROR   F. Welstead   London   nd   128
    TALES OF THE UNCANNY   Panther   1962   128
    WEIRD AND OCCULT MISCELLANY   Swan   nd   105
Asquith, Cynthia (Editor)
    THE SECOND GHOST BOOK   Pan Books   1956   223
        Book: same
Bachelor, George C.
    UNCANNY   Mitre Press   1945   32
Barrett, William E.
    THE FOOLS OF TIME   Pocket Books   1964   309
Blackwood, Algernon
    THE CENTAUR   Penguin   Middlesex, England   1938   280
        Book: same
    SELECTED TALES OF ALGERNON BLACKWOOD. STORIES OF THE SUPERNATURAL AND UNCAN
        Penguin   Middlesex, England   1942   173
Burroughs, Edgar Rice
    TARZAN AND THE CASTAWAYS   Ballantine   1965   191
        Book: same
Campbell, John W. (Editor)
    ANALOG I   Paperback Library   1964   160
        Book: same
Conway, Hugh
    DARK DAYS   Arrowsmith   London   1884   178
    THE SECRET OF THE STRADIVARIUS   Holerth Press   London   nd   73
Corelli, Marie
    THE STRANGE VISITATION OF JOSIAH MCNASON. A CHRISTMAS GHOST STORY
        G. Newnes   London   1904   118   Ill.

Crane, Walter B.
    ODD TALES   M. Witmark   New York and Chicago   1900   106
De Morgan, John
    IN UNKNOWN WORLDS; OR, A TRIP TO MYSTERY LAND   Street & Smith   1927   214
Doyle, A. Conan
    THE CAPTAIN OF THE POLE STAR   G. Munro   1895   95
        Book: same - title story only
Erckman, Emile and Chatrian, Alexandre
    FANTASTIC TALES OF THE RHINELAND   Dick's English Novels   nd   151
Hampden, John
    GHOST STORIES   Dent London   1960   366
Hardie, John L. (Editor)
    ANOTHER SEVEN STRANGE STORIES   Art & Educational   Glasgow   nd   80
    SEVEN STRANGE STORIES   Art & Educational   Glasgow   nd   80
    STRANGE STORIES, THE LAST SEVEN   Art & Educational   Glasgow   nd   80
Kennaway, James
    THE WIND BENDERS   Signet   1964   159
Henty, G. A.
    THE CAT OF BUBASTES   Street & Smith   1903   348
        Book: same
Hume, Fergus
    THE DWARF'S CHAMBER   New Amsterdam Book Co   1900   386
    THE YEAR OF THE MIRACLE. A MARVELLOUS TALE OF A STRANGE PLAGUE
        Street & Smith   1903   187
        Book: same
Irish, William
    IF I SHOULD DIE BEFORE I WAKE   Avon   1943   128
James, G. P. R.
    THE CASTLE OF EHRENSTEIN; ITS LORDS SPIRITUAL AND TEMPORAL; ITS INHABITANTS
    EARTHLY AND UNEARTHLY   Harper   1847   138
        Book: same
Kingsford, Anna
    DREAMS AND DREAM STORIES   F. Lovell   1889   281
Knight, Damon (Editor)
    TOMORROW X 4   Fawcett   1964   176
Leiber, Maxim
    GHOSTS, GHOULS AND OTHER NUISANCES   Seven Seas   Berlin   1959   265
Linskill, W. T.
    ST. ANDREWS GHOST STORIES   Innes   London   1936   117
Machen, Arthur
    THE GREAT GOD PAN AND OTHER WEIRD TALES   Armed Forces Edition   1946   229
        Book: same
Marsh, Richard
    THE BEETLE   World Distributors   London   nd   252
        Book: same
    THE MYSTERY OF THE BEETLE; OR, THE HOUSE WITH THE OPEN WINDOW
        Westlake   Cleveland   1912   310
        Book: THE BEETLE
Meade, L. T. and Halifax, Clifford, M. D.
    STORIES FROM THE DIARY OF A DOCTOR: 2nd SERIES   Sands   London   1901   122

"A" MEN Le Page
THE ABOMINABLE EARTHMAN Pohl
ACCOUNT OF A RACE OF HUMAN BEINGS WITH TAILS   Anonymous
ACROSS THE AGES Statten
ACROSS TIME Grinnell
ADAM AND EVE AND PINCH ME Coppard
ADAM LINK IN THE PAST Binder
ADDRESS: CENTAURI Wallace
ADRIFT IN A BONEYARD Taylor
ADRIFT IN THE UNKNOWN Cook
AN ADVENTURE IN VENUS Science Fiction Series #3
ADVENTURES IN THE FAR FUTURE Wollheim
ADVENTURES IN TIME AND SPACE Healy and McComas
THE ADVENTURES OF LANCELOT BIGGS Bond
ADVENTURES ON OTHER PLANETS Wollheim
ADVISE AND CONSENT Drury
THE AERIEL WAR Rowe
AFTER DOOMSDAY Anderson
AFTER MANY A SUMMER DIES THE SWAN Huxley
AFTER THE ATOM La Salle
AFTER THE RAIN Bowen
AFTERMATH Berry
AGENT OF THE UNKNOWN St. Clair
AGENT OF VEGA Schmitz
AGAINST THE FALL OF NIGHT Clarke
AHEAD OF TIME Kuttner
ALAS, BABYLON Frank
ALICE IN RANKBUSTLAND Otterbourge
ALICE IN WONDERLAND Carroll
ALICE'S ADVENTURES IN CAMBRIDGE Evarts
THE ALIEN Jones
ALIEN Muller
ALIEN FROM ARCTURUS Dickson
ALIEN IMPACT Tubb
THE ALIEN ONES Brett
ALIEN PLANET Pratt
ALIEN UNIVERSE Gridban
ALIEN WORLDS Elwood
THE ALIENS Leinster
ALL THE TRAPS OF EARTH Simak
ALLAN QUATERMAIN Haggard
THE ALLEY GOD Farmer
ALMURIC Howard
ALONE BY NIGHT Congdon
ALPHA CENTAURI OR DIE Brackett
ALPHA YES, TERRA NO! Petaja
THE ALTAR OF ASCONEL Brunner
THE ALTERED EGO Sohl
ALTERNATING CURRENTS Pohl
AMATEURS IN ALCHEMY Deegan
THE AMERICAN FAUST Paulton
AMOROUS PHILANDRE De Bibiena
THE AMPHIBIANS Wright
ANALOG I Campbell

ANALOGUE MEN Knight
AND SOME WERE HUMAN del Rey
AND THE STARS REMAIN Berry
AND THEN THE TOWN TOOK OFF Wilson
THE ANDES TRAIL Radford
ANDROID Zeigfried
ANDROID AVENGER White
THE ANGELIC AVANGERS Andrezel
THE ANGRY ESPERS Biggle
ANIMAL FARM Orwell
ANNIHILATION! Statten
ANOTHER KIND Oliver
ANOTHER SEVEN STRANGE STORIES Hardie
ANOTHER SPACE--ANOTHER TIME Campbell
ANTHEM Rand
ANTI-GAS! Simpson
ANTRO, THE LIFE-GIVER Deegan
APACHE DEVIL Burroughs
APE AND ESSENCE Huxley
THE APE AND THE DIAMOND Marsh
THE APE OF GOD Holesworth
APE-MAN'S OFFERING Kaner
APHRODITE Louys
APOLLO AT GO Sutton
ARCHY AND MEHITABEL Marquis
ARCTIC BRIDE Meek
"ARGENTIS" Shaw
ARMAGEDDON: 2419 A. D. Nowlan
ARROW BOOK OF GHOST STORIES Kramer
THE ARSENAL OF MIRACLES Fox
AS IT WAS WRITTEN Speight
ASSAULT FROM INFINITY La Salle
ASSIGNMENT IN ETERNITY Heinlein
ASSIGNMENT TO DISASTER Aarons
ASTEROID FORMA Le Page
ASTEROID MAN Fanthorpe
ASTOUNDING SCIENCE FICTION ANTHOLOGY Campbell
ASTOUNDING TALES OF SPACE AND TIME Campbell
ASTRO RACE Lang
THE ASTRONAUTS MUST NOT LAND Brunner
AT THE EARTH'S CORE Burroughs
ATLAS SHRUGGED Rand
THE ATLANTIC ABOMINATION Brunner
ATLANTIDA Benoit
THE ATOM CLOCK Lengyel
THE ATOM CURTAIN Williams
ATOMIC BOMB Jameson
ATOMIC NEMESIS Zeigfried
ATOMS AND EVIL Bloch
ATOMS IN ACTION Sheldon
ATOM-WAR ON MARS Tubb
ATTA Bellamy
THE AUSTRAL GLOBE Ramsey
THE AUTOMATED GOLIATH Temple

THE AVENGING MARTIAN Statton
THE AVENGING NOTE Science Fiction Series #17
THE AVENGING RAY Seamark
AVON GHOST READER Anonymous
AVON MYSTERY STORYTELLER Anonymous
AVON STORY TELLER Anonymous
AWAY AND BEYOND van Vogt
AZAR THE MIGHTY Hardy

BABIES WITHOUT TAILS Duranty
BACK TO THE STONE AGE Burroughs
BAR THE DOORS Hitchcock
BARON MUNCHAUSEN Raspe
BARRIER 346 Zeigfried
BARRIER UNKNOWN Merak
BATTLE FOR THE STARS Hamilton
THE BATTLE OF THE SINGING MEN Kersh
THE BATTLE OF THE SWASH Barton
BATTLE ON VENUS Temple
BEACHHEADS IN SPACE Derleth
THE BEAST van Vogt
THE BEAST MASTER Norton
THE BEASTS FROM BEYOND Wellman
THE BEASTS OF TARZAN Burroughs
THE BEETLE Marsh
BEFORE THE BEGINNING Reiser
BENITA Haggard
BEST AMERICAN SHORT STORIES 1955 Foley
BEST FROM FANTASY AND SCIENCE FICTION: 3rd Series Boucher and McComas
BEST FROM FANTASY AND SCIENCE FICTION: 4th Series Boucher
BEST FROM FANTASY AND SCIENCE FICTION: 5th Series Boucher
BEST FROM FANTASY AND SCIENCE FICTION: 6th Series Boucher
BEST FROM FANTASY AND SCIENCE FICTION: 7th Series Boucher
BEST FROM FANTASY AND SCIENCE FICTION: 8th Series Boucher
BEST FROM FANTASY AND SCIENCE FICTION: 9th Series Mills
BEST FROM FANTASY AND SCIENCE FICTION: 10th Series Mills
THE BEST FROM NEW WORLDS Carnell
BEST GHOST STORIES Le Fanu
BEST GHOST STORIES Ridler
BEST S F Crispin
BEST S F TWO Crispin
BEST STORIES Wells
BETWEEN PLANETS Heinlein
BETWEEN WORLDS Smith
BEYOND Bradbury, Sturgeon
BEYOND Sturgeon
BEYOND EARTH'S GATES Padget and Moore
BEYOND EDEN Duncan
BEYOND GEO Romilus
BEYOND HUMAN KNE Merril
BEYOND INFINITY Carr
BEYOND THE BARRIER Knight
BEYOND THE END OF TIME Pohl
BEYOND THE FARTHEST STAR Burroughs

BEYOND THE FOURTH DOOR Deegan
   BEYOND THE GALACTIC RIM Chandler
BEYOND THE GALAXY Zeigfried
BEYOND THE MOON Hamilton
BEYOND THE NIGHT Woolrich
BEYOND THE SEAS Stamper
BEYOND THE SILVER SKY Bulmer
BEYOND THE SOLAR SYSTEM Haley
BEYOND THE STARS Cummings
BEYOND THE VANISHING POINT Cummings
BEYOND THE VEIL Thanet
BEYOND THE VOID Muller
BEYOND THESE SUNS Le Page
BEYOND TIME Muller
BEYOND TIME AND SPACE Derleth
BEYOND ZOASTER Charles
THE BIG BALL OF WAX Mead
THE BIG BOOK OF SCIENCE FICTION Conklin
THE BIG EYE Ehrlich
THE BIG JUMP Brackett
BIG PLANET Vance
THE BIG TIME Leiber
BILLENIUM Ballard
THE BILLIONAIRE McGowan
BIOLOGY "A" Kent
BIO-MUTON Elliot
THE BIRD OF TIME West
THE BISHOP'S JAEGERS Smith
BITTER REFLECTION Fanthorpe
BLACK ABYSS Powers
BLACK AUGUST Wheatley
THE BLACK AVENGER Statten
BLACK BARGAIN Statten
THE BLACK CASTLE; OR, THE SPECTRE OF THE FOREST Anonymous
THE BLACK CLOUD Hoyle
THE BLACK FLAME Weinbaum
THE BLACK GALAXY Leinster
BLACK INFINITY Brett
BLACK INFINITY Cameron
THE BLACK SPHERE La Salle
BLACK WING OF MARS Statten
BLAGUE Duane and Leverentz
THE BLIND SPOT Hall and Flint
THE BLOODY SUN Bradley
BLUE ASP Le Page
THE BLUE ATOM Williams
BLUE CORDON Carter
BLUE PERIL Barry
THE BLUE RAY George
THE BODY SNATCHERS Finney
BODYGUARD Gold
BOGEY MEN Bloch
BOMBS IN ORBIT Sutton
A BOOK OF STRANGE STORIES van Thal

BORN OF LUNA Statten
BOW DOWN TO NUL Aldiss
THE BOY IN BLACK Thorpe
THE BRAIN OF THE PLANET Science Fiction Series #5
BRAIN PALAEO Romilus
THE BRAIN STEALERS Leinster
BRAIN TWISTER Phillips
BRAIN ULTIMATE Campbell
BRAIN WAVE Anderson
THE BRAINS OF HELLE Mistral
A BRAND NEW WORLD Cummings
THE BRAND OF THE WEREWOLF Robeson
THE BRASS BOTTLE Anstey
BRAVE NEW WORLD Huxley
BRAVE NEW WORLD REVISITED Huxley
BRIDE OF FU MANCHU Rohmer
THE BRIDES OF DRACULA Owen
BRIDES OF THE DEVIL Yorke
BRIGANDS OF THE MOON Campbell
BRIGANDS OF THE MOON Cummings
THE BRIGHT PHOENIX Mead
BRING BACK YESTERDAY Chandler
BRING THE JUBILEE Moore
THE BROTHER OF THE SHADOW Praed
BR-R-R! Conklin
BUDRY'S INFERNO Budrys
BUN-BUKU CHAGAMA Sazanami
THE BURIED WORLD Day
BURN WITCH, BURN Merritt
THE BURNING COURT Carr
BURNING VOID Magroon
THE BURNING WORLD Ballard
BUSH CLAWS Garon
BYPASS TO OTHERNESS Kuttner

THE CACHE FROM OUTER SPACE Farmer
THE CADAVER OF GIDEON WYCK Laing
THE CALL OF THE HAND Golding
CALL OF THE WILD Fanthorpe
CANARY IN A CAT HOUSE Vonnegut
A CANTICLE FOR LEIBOWITZ Miller
THE CAPTAIN OF THE LOCUSTS Werner
THE CAPTAIN OF THE POLE STAR Doyle
CAPTIVE ON THE FLYING SAUCER Finn
CAPTIVES OF THE FLAME Delany
CARAVAN OF CRIME O'Donnell
CARSON OF VENUS Burroughs
THE CASE AGAINST TOMORROW Pohl
THE CASE OF CHARLES DEXTER WARD Lovecraft
A CASE OF CONSCIENCE Blish
THE CASE OF THE MISSING AIRMAN Elliott
CAST AWAY AT THE POLE Cook
CASTAWAY Cozzens
CASTAWAY FROM SPACE Brack

CASTAWAY'S WORLD Brunner
THE CASTLE OF EHRENSTEIN James
CASTLE OF IRON de Camp and Pratt
THE CASTLE OF OTRANTO Walpole
CASTLE SKULL Carr
THE CAT OF BUBASTES Henty
CATACLYSM Statten
CATALYST Kent
THE CATALYST Statten
CATSEYE Norton
CAVIAR Sturgeon
CAVE-BOY EREK Dundee
THE CAVE GIRL Burroughs
THE CAVES OF DEATH Norwood
THE CAVES OF STEEL Asimov
THE CELESTIAL BLUEPRINT Farmer
THE CENTAUR Blackwood
CENTURION'S VENGEANCE Fanthorpe
A CENTURY OF SCIENCE FICTION Knight
THE CHANGELING WORLDS Bulmer
CHAOS Bell
THE CHAOS FIGHTERS Williams
CHAOS IN ARCTURUS Zeigfried
CHAOS IN MINIATURE Campbell
CHAOS IS COME AGAIN Houghton
CHARIOT INTO TIME Zeigfried
CHESSBOARD PLANET Padgett
THE CHESSMEN OF MARS Burroughs
CHEZ ROBERT Marlowe
CHILDHOOD'S END Clarke
CHILDREN OF THE ATOM Shiras
CHLOROPLASM Carter
A CHRISTMAS CAROL Dickens
CHRONICLES OF SIMON CHRISTIANUS Fidel
THE CIRCUS OF DR. LAO Bradbury
THE CIRCUS OF DR. LAO Finney
CITIZEN IN SPACE Sheckley
CITY Simak
THE CITY AND THE STARS Clarke
THE CITY AT WORLD'S END Hamilton
CITY IN THE SEA Tucker
CITY OF A THOUSAND SUNS Delany
CITY OF GLASS Loomis
CITY OF NO RETURN Tubb
CITY ON THE MOON Leinster
CITY UNDER THE SEA Bulmer
CITY UNDER THE SEA Fairman
THE CIVIL WAR OF 1915 Brex
CLANS OF THE ALPHANE MOON Dick
CLEOPATRA'S NIGHTS Barnard
THE CLIMACTICON Livingston
THE CLOCK STRIKES TWELVE Wakefield
CLOSE TO CRITICAL Clement
THE COILS OF TIME Chandler

COLD COMFORT FARM Gibbons
COLLECTED WRITINGS Bierce
COLLISION COURSE Silverberg
THE COLORS OF SPACE Bradley
THE COLOUR OUT OF SPACE Lovecraft
THE COMPLETE SHORT STORIES Twain
CONAN THE CONQUEROR Howard
CONDITIONALLY HUMAN Miller
CONJURE WIFE Leiber
A CONNECTICUT YANKEE IN KING ARTHUR'S COURT Twain
CONQUERORS OF VENUS Kennedy
CONQUEST OF EARTH Banister
CONQUEST OF THE SPACE SEA Williams
CONQUEST OF THE STARS Leinster
CONTRABAND ROCKET Correy
THE CORAL ISLAND Reynolds
CORPUS EARTHLING Charbonneau
CORRIDORS OF TIME Deegan
COSMIC CHECKMATE DeVet and MacLean
THE COSMIC COMPUTER Piper
COSMIC CONQUEST Blair
COSMIC ECHELON Cameron
COSMIC EXODUS Holt
THE COSMIC FLAME Statten
COSMIC MANHUNT de Camp
THE COSMIC PUPPETS Dick
THE COSMIC RAPE Sturgeon
COSMOPOLITANS Maugham
COSTIGAN'S NEEDLE Sohl
CRASHING SUNS Woodcott
THE CREATION Science Fiction Series #9
THE CREATOR Simak
CREATURES OF THE ABYSS Leinster
CREEP, SHADOW, CREEP Merritt
CREEPS BY NIGHT Hammett
CRIME FLIES Luigi
CRIMSON PLANET Muller
CRISIS IN 2140 Piper and McGuire
THE CROSS ON THE DRUM Cave
CROSSROADS IN TIME Conklin
THE CROSSROADS OF TIME Norton
CRY HORROR Lovecraft
CRY OF THE BEAST Norwood
THE CRYSTAL BUTTON Thomas
A CUPFUL OF SPACE Clingerman
THE CURRENTS OF SPACE Asimov
THE CURSE OF KA Farnshaw
CURSE OF THE PLANET KUZ van Loden
CURSE OF THE TOTEM Fanthorpe
THE COUNT DE LAPOUR Watson
CYCLE OF FIRE Clement
CYBERNETIC CONTROLLER Clarke and Bulmer

D-99 Fyfe
THE DAMNED Talbot
DANGEROUS LOVE Farley
DARBY O'GILL AND THE LITTLE PEOPLE Watkins
DARE Farmer
DARK ANDROMEDA Merak
THE DARK BEASTS Long
DARK BOUNDARIES Lorraine
DARK CENTAURI Zeigfried
DARK CONFLICT Merak
DARK CONTINUUM Muller
DARK DAYS Conway
DARK DECEMBER Coppel
THE DARK DESTROYERS Wellman
DARK DOMINION Duncan
THE DARK GATEWAY Burke
THE DARK INTRUDER Bradley
DARK SIDE OF VENUS Macartney
DARK UNIVERSE Galouye
THE DARK WORLD Kuttner
THE DARKER DRINK Fanthorpe
DARKER THAN YOU THINK Williamson
DARKNESS AND THE DEEP Fisher
DARKNESS BEFORE TOMORROW Williams
A DASH TO THE POLE Ward
DAUGHTER OF FU MANCHU Rohmer
DAVY Pangborn
DAWN OF DARKNESS del Martia
DAWN OF THE MUTANTS Roberts
THE DAY AFTER TOMORROW Heinlein
THE DAY KRUSCHEV PANICKED Mair
THE DAY NEW YORK WENT DRY Einstein
DAY OF THE BEASTS Muller
DAY OF THE GIANTS del Rey
THE DAY OF THE TRIFFIDS Wyndham
THE DAY THE EARTH CAUGHT FIRE Wells
THE DAY THE EARTH FROZE Hatch
THE DAY THE OCEANS OVERFLOWED Fontenay
THE DAY THE WORLD DIED Muller
THE DAY THE WORLD ENDED Rohmer
THE DAY THEY H-BOMBED LOS ANGELES Williams
THE DAY THEY INVADED NEW YORK Lewis
DAYBREAK: 2250 A. D. Norton
DE BRACY'S DRUG Gridban
DEADLINE TO PLUTO Statten
DEADLY IMAGE Cooper
DEADLY LITTER White
DEALS WITH THE DEVIL Davenport
DEATH AND HIS SWEETHEART Duke
THE DEATH BELL Marshall
DEATH DIMENSION Barry
DEATH HAS NO WEIGHT Luigi
DEATH HAS TWO FACES Fanthorpe
DEATH OF A WORLD Farjeon

DEATH OF THE MOON Phillips
DEATH OF THE VAMPIRE BARONESS Van der Elst
DEATH RAY DICTATOR Titterton
DEATH WARRIORS Garon
DEATHWORLD Harrison
DEATHWORLD II Harrison
DECREATION Statten
DEEP FREEZE Butler
THE DEEP RANGE Clarke
DEEP SPACE Russell
THE DEFIANT AGENTS Norton
DEFY THE FOUL FIEND Collier
THE DELICATE APE Hughes
THE DELUGE da Vinci
THE DELUGE Wright
DELUSION WORLD Dickson
THE DEMOLISHED MAN Bester
DEMON'S WORLD Bulmer
DEPTHS OF DEATH Luigi
THE DESIRE OF THE EYES Allen
DESPOT OF THE WORLD Rochester
DESTINATION ALPHA Cameron
DESTINATION MARS Brown
DESTINATION: UNIVERSE Van Vogt
DESTINATION: INFINITY Kuttner
DESTINY TIMES THREE Leiber
DESTINY'S ORBIT Grinnell
DESTROY THE U. S. A. Jenkins
THE DEVIATES Jones
THE DEVIL FROM THE DEPTHS Fanthorpe
THE DEVIL IN VELVET Carr
THE DEVIL RIDES OUT Wheatley
THE DEVIL WORSHIPPERS Lucky
DEVIL'S PLANET Wellman
THE DEVOURING FIRE Statten
DIABOLICAL GENIUS Le Fanu
DIALOGUES OF THE DEAD Lyttleton
DID SHE FALL? Smith
DIMENSION 4 Conklin
DIMENSION OF HORROR Bounds
THE DIPLOIDS MacLean
THE DISAPPEARANCE Wylie
THE DISSENTIZENS Condray
DIVIDE AND RULE de Camp
THE "DIVING DUCK" Miall
DOCTOR TO THE STARS Leinster
DR. BERKELEY'S DISCOVERY Slee
DR. BLOODMONEY Dick
DR. FUTURITY Dick
DR. KRASINSKI'S SECRET Shiel
A DOG'S HEAD Dutourd
THE DOLL MAKER Sarban
DOME AROUND AMERICA Williamson
DOME WORLD McLaughlin

DOOMED NATION OF THE SKIES Future
DOOMSDAY Scott
DOOMSDAY EVE Williams
DOOMSDAY MORNING Moore
DOOMSDAY, 1999 MacTyre
THE DOOMSTONE Woolrich
DONOVAN'S BRAIN Siodmak
THE DOOR INTO SUMMER Heinlein
DOOR THROUGH SPACE Bradley
DOUBLE JEOPARDY Pratt
THE DOUBLE SHADOW Smith
DOUBLE STAR Heinlein
DOWN AMAZON WAY Marks
DRACULA Stoker
THE DRAGON MASTERS Vance
DRAGON'S ISLAND Williamson
DREAD OF NIGHT O'Donnell
DREAD VISITOR Berry
DREADFUL HOLLOW Karlova
DREADFUL SANCTUARY Russell
THE DREAM QUEST OF UNKNOWN KADATH Lovecraft
THE DREAMING EARTH Brunner
THE DREAMING SKULL Safroni-Middleton
DREAMS AND DREAM STORIES Kingsford
THE DREAM-WOMAN Collins
THE DROWNED WORLD Ballard
THE DRUMS OF FU MANCHU Rohmer
DRUNKARD'S WALK Pohl
DUEL IN NIGHTMARE WORLDS Flackes
THE DUNWICH HORROR Lovecraft
THE DUPLICATED MAN Blish and Lowndes
THE DUPLICATORS Leinster
THE DUST DESTROYERS Statten
THE DWARF'S CHAMBER Hume
DWELLERS IN SPACE Reed
DWELLERS IN THE MIRAGE Merritt
THE DYBBUK Ansky
THE DYING EARTH Vance
DYNASTY OF DOOM Grey
THE DYNO DEPRESSANT Gridban

E PLURIBUS UNICORN Sturgeon
EARTH ABIDES Stewart
THE EARTH GODS ARE COMING Bulmer
AN EARTH GONE MAD Dee
THE EARTH IN PERIL Wollheim
THE EARTH INVASION BATTALION Hughes
EARTH IS ROOM ENOUGH Asimov
EARTH OUR NEW EDEN Rayer
EARTH REVISITED Brooks
THE EARTH WAR Reynolds
EARTH-BORN Gentil
EARTHLIGHT Clarke
EARTHMAN, COME HOME Blish

EARTHMAN GO HOME Anderson
AN EARTHMAN ON VENUS Farley
THE EARTHQUAKE-MAKER Roberts
EARTH'S LAST CITADEL Moore and Kuttner
THE EATER OF DARKNESS Coates
THE ECLIPSE EXPRESS Statten
ECHO IN THE SKULL Brunner
ECHO X Barzman
THE ECHOING WORLDS Burke
EDGE OF ETERNITY Muller
EDGE OF TIME Grinnell
EDGE OF TOMORROW Fast
EIGHT KEYS TO EDEN Clifton
8th ANNUAL EDITION THE YEAR'S BEST S F Merril
THE EIGHTH WONDER Cook
ELEKTRON UNION Hunt
THE ELIXIR Science Fiction Series #10
ELLISON WONDERLAND Ellison
EMPEROR FU MANCHU Rohmer
EMPEROR OF MARS Fearn
EMPIRE Simak
EMPIRE OF SHAOS Bulmer
EMPIRE OF THE ATOM van Vogt
ENCOUNTER Folly
ENCOUNTER IN SPACE Bulmer
THE END OF ETERNITY Asimov
END OF THE WORLD Owen
THE END OF THE WORLD Wollheim
THE ENDLESS SHADOW Brunner
THE ENEMY STARS Anderson
ENTERPRISE 2115 Grey
ENVOY TO NEW WORLDS Laumer
EPEDEMIC Slaughter
EREWHON Butler
ESCAPE ON VENUS Burroughs
THE ESCAPE ORBIT White
ESCAPE TO EARTH Howard
ESCAPE TO EDEN Pratt
ESCAPE TO INFINITY Zeigfried
ESCAPE TO NOWHERE Karp
ESPER Blish
THE ETERNAL MOMENT Forster
THE ETERNAL SAVAGE Burroughs
EXILE FROM XANADU Wright
THE EXILE OF TIME Cummings
EXILES IN TIME Deegan
EXILES OF TIME Bond
EXIT HUMANITY Brett
EXIT LIFE Gridban
THE EXORCISTS Muller
EXPEDITION TO EARTH Clarke
THE EXPLORERS Kornbluth
EYE IN THE SKY Dick
THE EYE OF KARNAK Muller

EYE OF THE MONSTER Norton
EYELESS IN GAZA Huxley

THE FABULOUS VALLEY Wheatley
THE FACE IN THE ABYSS Merritt
FACE IN THE DARK Fanthorpe
FACE IN THE NIGHT Brett
FACE OF EVIL Fanthorpe
THE FACE OF FEAR Torro
THE FACE THAT LAUNCHED A THOUSAND SHIPS Kelley
FAHRENHEIT 451 Bradbury
FALCONS OF NARABEDLA Bradley
THE FALL. A TALE OF EDEN Searel
A FALL OF MOONDUST Clarke
THE FALL OF THE HOUSE OF USHER Poe
THE FALLING TORCH Budrys
FALSE NIGHT Budrys
FAMOUS SCIENCE FICTION STORIES Healy and McComas
FANCIES AND GOODNIGHTS Collier
FANTASTIC TALES OF THE RHINELAND Erckman and Chatrian
FAR AND AWAY Boucher
FAR BEYOND THE BLUE Amper
FAR OUT Knight
THE FATAL FOCUS Valdez
THE FATAL LAW Kent
FEAR Hubbard
FEAR AND TREMBLING Hitchcock
THE FEAR MAKERS Teilhet
FEE, FEI, FO, FUM Aylesworth
THE FELLOWSHIP OF THE RING Tolkien
THE FEMALE DEMON McDougle
FERRY ROCKET Kinley
THE FIEND IN YOU Beaumont
5th ANNUAL YEAR'S BEST S F Merril
THE FIFTH GALAXY READER Gold
THE FIFTY MINUTE HOUR Lindner
FIGHT FOR LIFE Leinster
FIGHTING AGAINST MILLIONS Carter
A FIGHTING MAN OF MARS Burroughs
FIGMENT OF A DREAM Keller
THE FINAL WAR Keller
FINGERS OF DARKNESS Fanthorpe
FIRE IN THE HEAVENS Smith
FIRE PAST THE FUTURE Maine
THE FIRE GODDESS Rohmer
FIRE WATCHER'S NIGHT Kaner
FIRST FLIGHT Knight
FIRST HE DIED Simak
FIRST LENSMAN Smith
THE FIRST MEN IN THE MOON Wells
FIRST ON MARS Gordon
FIRST ON THE MOON Sutton
FIRST ON THE MOON Walters
FIRST THROUGH TIME Gordon

FIRST TO THE STARS Gordon
FISSION Hunt
FIVE FACES OF FEAR Rhorpe
FIVE GALAXY SHORT NOVELS Gold
THE FIVE GOLD BANDS Vance
FIVE ODD Conklin
5 TALES FROM TOMORROW Dikty
FIVE WEEKS IN A BALLOON Fox
FLAME MASS Fanthorpe
FLATLAND Abbott
FLESH Farmer
FLIGHT FROM YESTERDAY Williams
FLIGHT INTO SPACE Wollheim
THE FLIGHT OF THE AEROFIX Science Fiction Series #14
FLIGHT OF THE "HESPER" Hay
THE FLYING EYES Holly
THE FLYING FISH Beresford
THE FLYING YORKSHIREMAN Knight
THE FOOD OF THE GODS Wells
THE FOOLS OF TIME Barrett
THE FORBIDDEN Brett
FORBIDDEN PLANET Muller
FORBIDDEN PLANET Stuart
FORCE 97-X Torro
THE FOREVER MACHINE Clifton and Riley
THE FORGOTTEN PLANET Leinster
FORMULA FOR POWER Batt
FORMULA 29X Torro
FORMULA 895 Hughes
FOUR FOR THE FUTURE Conklin
FOUR FROM PLANET FIVE Leinster
THE FOUR SIDED TRIANGLE Temple
THE FOURTH GALAXY READER Gold
THE FOURTH "R" Smith
14 OF MY FAVORITES IN SUSPENSE Hitchcock
43,000 YEARS LATER Coon
THE FOX WOMAN Merritt
FRANCIS Stern
FRANKENSTEIN Shelley
THE FRANKENSTEIN READER Beck
THE FREEZING PERIL STRIKES Luigi
FRIGHT Collins
FROM EARTH'S CENTER Welcome
FROM OUTER SPACE Clement
FROM POLE TO POLE Stables
FROM REALMS BEYOND Brett
FROM THE EARTH TO THE MOON Verne
FROM WHAT FAR STAR? Berry
FRONTIERS IN SPACE Bleiler and Dikty
THE FROZEN LIMIT Gridban
THE FROZEN PIRATE Russell
THE FROZEN TOMB Brett
THE FROZEN YEAR Blish
FUGITIVE OF THE STARS Hamilton

FUGITIVE OF TIME Grey
FULL MOON Mundy
FULLY DRESSED AND IN HIS RIGHT MIND Fessier
THE FUNHOUSE Appel
FURY Kuttner
THE FURY FROM EARTH McLaughlin
FUTURE TENSE Vance
THE G-BOMB Statten
GABRIEL OVER THE WHITE HOUSE Tweed
THE GALACTIC BREED Brackett
GALACTIC CLUSTER Blish
GALACTIC DERELICT Norton
GALACTIC INTRIGUE Bulmer
GALACTIC PATROL Smith
GALACTIC STORM Hunt
GALAXIES LIKE GRAINS OF SAND Aldiss
GALAXY OF GHOULS Merril
THE GALAXY PRIMES Smith
GALAXY 666 Torro
THE GAME PLAYERS OF TITAN Dick
THE GAMES OF NEITH St. Clair
GAMMA PRODUCT Barry
GAMMA RAY MURDERS Yorke
THE GARDEN OF FEAR Howard
GATEWAY TO ELSEWHERE Leinster
GATHER, DARKNESS Leiber
THE GENETIC GENERAL Dickson
THE GENIAL DINOSAUR Gridban
GENUS HOMO de Camp and Miller
GET OUT OF MY SKY Margulies
GHOST AND HORROR STORIES Beirce
THE GHOST BOOK Asquith
GHOST STORIES Hampden
GHOST STORIES OF AN ANTIQUARY James
GHOST TALES Brown
GHOSTS AND THINGS Cantor
GHOSTS DON'T KILL Valdez
GHOSTS, GHOULS AND OTHER NUISANCES Leiber
THE GHOSTS OF MANACLE Finney
THE GHOUL AND THE GODDESS Fane
THE GHOUL KEEPERS Margulies
THE GIRL FROM MARS Science Fiction Series #1
GIRL IN TROUBLE Parker
THE GIRL WITH THE HUNGRY EYES Anonymous
THE GIRLS FROM PLANET 5 Wilson
GLADIATOR Wylie
GLADIATOR-AT-LAW Pohl and Kornbluth
THE GLASS BEES Juenger
THE GLORIOUS POOL Smith
THE GLORY ROAD Heinlein
THE GLOWING GLOBE Luigi
THE GOBLIN TOWER Long
GODDESS OF MARS Fearn
GODDESS OF NIGHT Fanthorpe

GODLING, GO HOME Silverberg
THE GODS HATE KANSAS Millard
GODS OF DARKNESS Zeigfried
THE GODS OF MARS Burroughs
THE GOLD OF AKADA Titan
THE GOLD WORSHIPPERS Author of "Whitefriars"
THE GOLDEN APPLES OF THE SUN Bradbury
THE GOLDEN ARGOSY Cartmill and Grayson
THE GOLDEN ASS Apuleius
GOLDEN BLOOD Williamson
THE GOLDEN CHALICE Fanthorpe
THE GOLDEN KAZOO Schneider
THE GOLDEN PEOPLE Saberhagen
THE GOLDEN ROOMS Fisher
THE GOLDEN SCORPION Rohmer
THE GOLDEN WIND Ohta and Sperry
GORGO Bingham
GOTHIC PIECES Anonymous Anthology
THE GRASS AND A TREE OF NIGHT Capote
THE GRASS IS ALWAYS GREENER Malcolm-Smith
GRAVEYARD OF THE DAMNED Fanthorpe
THE GRAVEYARD READER Conklin
THE GRAND ILLUSION Statten
THE GREAT DISASTER Bredon
THE GREAT EXPLOSION Russell
GREAT GHOST STORIES Stern
THE GREAT GOD PAN Machen
THE GREAT MIRROR Burks
THE GREAT ONES Deegan
THE GREAT RED DRAGON Chester
GREAT SCIENCE FICTION ADVENTURES Shaw
GREAT SCIENCE FICTION BY SCIENTISTS Conklin
GREAT TALES AND POEMS Poe
THE GREATEST ADVENTURE Taine
THE GREEN GIRL Williamson
THE GREEN HILLS OF EARTH Heinlein
THE GREEN MAN Sherman
THE GREEN MANDARIN MYSTERY Malcolm
GREEN MANSIONS Hudson
THE GREEN MARE Ayme
THE GREEN MILLENNIUM Leiber
THE GREEN ODYSSEY Farmer
THE GREEN PLANET Holly
THE GREEN QUEEN St. Clair
THE GREEN RAIN Tabori
GREEN THOUGHTS Collier
GREENER THAN YOU THINK Moore
THE GREEKS BRING GIFTS Leinster
THE GREY BEAST Atholl
GREYBEARD Aldiss
GRIFFIN BOOKLET ONE Wells and North
THE GRIM CARETAKER Ascher
THE GRIP OF FEAR Fanthorpe
GUARDIANS OF TIME Anderson

GULLIVER OF MARS Arnold
GULLIVER'S TRAVELS Swift
GUNNER CADE Judd
GYRATOR CONTROL Lang
"H" FOR HORRIFIC Miller
THE HAMELIN PLAGUE Chandler
HAND OF DOOM Fanthorpe
THE HAND OF FU MANCHU Rohmer
HAND OF GLORY Herbert
HAND OF HAVOC Grey
THE HAND OF ZEI de Camp
A HANDFUL OF TIME Brown
HANGOVER HOUSE Rohmer
THE HAPLOIDS Sohl
HARTAS MATURIN Lester
THE HAUNTED HOMESTEAD Southworth
THE HAUNTED HOTEL Collins
THE HAUNTED STARS Hamilton
THE HAUNTING OF TOBY JUG Wheatley
HE, A COMPANION TO SHE Anonymous
HE OWNED THE WORLD Maine
THE HELL FRUIT Rose
HELL HAS WINGS Fanthorpe
HELL PLANET Tubb
HELL SHIPS OF MANY WATERS O'Donnell
HELLFLOWER Smith
HELL'S PAVEMENT Knight
HERO'S WALK Crane
THE HIDDEN LAND Roberts
THE HIDDEN PLANET Wollheim
HIDDEN WORLD Coblentz
THE HIGH CRUSADE Anderson
HIGH VACUUM Maine
HIS FIRST MILLION WOMEN Weston
THE HISTORIES OF GARGANTUA AND PANTAGRUEL Rabelais
THE HOBBIT Tolkien
THE HOCUS ROOT Foster
HOLD YOUR BREATH Hitchcock
HOLY TERRORS Machen
HONEYMOON IN HELL Brown
THE HORROR EXPERT Long
HORROR MEDLEY Hervey
HORROR PARADE Hopkins
HORROR - 7 Bloch
HORROR STORIES Anonymous
HOSPITAL STATION White
HOSTILE WORLDS Hunt
HOT SWAG Kaner
THE HOUND OF DEATH Christie
THE HOUNDS OF TINDALOS Long
HOUSE OF ENTROPY Sheldon
HOUSE OF MANY CHANGES Reed
THE HOUSE OF MANY WORLDS Merwin
THE HOUSE ON THE BORDERLAND Hodgson
THE HOUSE THAT STOOD STILL van Vogt

THE HOUSES IF ISZM Vance
HOW GLASGOW CEASED TO FLOURISH Anonymous
HOW SLOW THE SMOOTH Herbert
HOW THE OLD WOMAN GOT HOME Shiel
THE HUGO WINNERS Asimov
HUMAN? Merril
HUMAN AND INHUMAN STORIES Sayers
THE HUMAN ANGLE Tenn
THE HUMAN BAT Home-Gall
THE HUMAN BAT V THE ROBOT GANGSTERS Home-Gall
HUMANOID PUPPETS Barry
THE HUMANOIDS Williamson
THE HUNGER Beaumont
I AM LEGEND Matheson
I AM THINKING OF MY DARLING McHugh
I CAME - I SAW - I WONDERED Gridban
I FIGHT FOR MARS Grey
I KILLED STALIN Noel
I, ROBOT Asimov
I SAW THREE SHIPS "Q"
I SPEAK FOR EARTH Woodcott
I WANT THE STARS Purdom
IF CHRIST CAME TO CONGRESS Howard
IF I SHOULD DIE BEFORE I WAKE Irish
IF THE SOUTH HAD WON THE CIVIL WAR Kantor
THE ILLUSTRATED MAN Bradbury
IMAGE OF DEATH Kensch
IMAGINATION UNLIMITED Bleiler and Dikty
THE IMITATION MAN Hargrave
IMMORTALITY, INC. Sheckley
THE IMMORTALS Brett
THE IMMORTALS Farley
THE IMMORTALS Garner
THE IMMORTALS Gunn
IMMORTALS OF MERCURY Science Fiction Series #16
IMPERIAL OVERTURE Hatfull
THE IMPOSSIBLES Phillips
IN AZTEC HANDS Heming
IN DEEP Knight
IN QUEST OF THE GOLDEN ORCHID Burton
IN THE BEGINNING Muller
IN THE DEAD OF NIGHT Sissons
IN THE GRIP OF TERROR Conklin
IN THE MIDST OF LIFE Bierce
IN THE WET Shute
IN UNKNOWN WORLDS De Morgan
THE INCOMPLETE ENCHANTER de Camp and Pratt
THE INDESTRUCTIBLE Garner
THE INDIAN SCOUT Aimard
INFERNO Statten
THE INFINITE MOMENT Wyndham
INFINITY MACHINE Muller
INNER COSMOS Statten
THE INSECT MEN Edgar

THE INSECT WARRIORS Levie
INSIDE, OUTSIDE Farmer
THE INSIDIOUS DR. FU MANCHU Rohmer
THE INTERLOPER Statten
INTERSTELLAR ESPIONAGE del Martia
INTO PLUTONIAN DEPTHS Coblentz
INTO THE ALTERNATE UNIVERSE Chandler
INTO THE FOURTH DIMENSION Cummings
THE INTRUDERS Fane
THE INVADERS ARE COMING Nourse and Meyer
INVADERS FROM EARTH Silverberg
INVADERS FROM RIGEL Pratt
INVADERS OF EARTH Conklin
INVADERS OF SPACE Leinster
THE INVADING ASTEROID Science Fiction Series #15
INVASION FROM MARS Welles
INVASION FROM SPACE Bradford
INVASION FROM 2500 Edwards
INVASION OF THE ROBOTS Elwood
THE INVISIBLE AVENGER Macrae
THE INVISIBLE COMPANION Farjeon
THE INVISIBLE MAN Wells
INVISIBLE MEN Davenport
THE IN-WORLD Roberts
IONIC BARRIER Kellar
IRISH FAIRY TALES AND STORIES Anonymous
THE ISLAND OF CAPTAIN SPARROW Wright
THE ISLAND OF CREEPING DEATH Norwood
THE ISLAND OF DR. MOREAU Wells
THE ISLAND OF FU MANCHU Rohmer
THE ISLAND OF THE DEAD Dunn
ISLANDIA Wright
ISLANDS IN THE SKY Clarke
THE ISLE OF PERIL Blake
"IT" A WILD, WEIRD HISTORY Anonymous
IT CAN'T HAPPEN HERE Lewis
IT HAPPENS EVERY SPRING Davies.
IT WAS THE DAY OF THE ROBOT Long
JACK OF EAGLES Blish
JAWS OF DEATH Ludwig
THE JEWEL OF THE SEVEN STARS Stoker
THE JEWELS OF APTOR Delany
JINN AND JITTERS Carnell
JOHN CARSTAIRS, SPACE DETECTIVE Long
JOHN CARTER OF MARS Burroughs
JOURNEY INTO SPACE Chilton
JOURNEY OF NIELS KLIM TO THE WORLD UNDERGROUND Holberg
JOURNEY TO MARS Tubb
JOURNEY TO THE CENTER OF THE EARTH Verne
THE JOY WAGON Hadley
JOYLEG Moore and Davidson
THE JOYMAKERS Gunn
JUDGMENT ON JANUS Norton
JUGGERNAUT Fane

JUNE IN THE VALLEY OF MONSTERS Buley
JUNGLE ALLIES Garon
THE JUNGLE BOOKS Kipling
JUNGLE TALES OF TARZAN Burroughs
JURGEN Cabell
THE KA OF GIFFORD HILLARY Wheatley
KACHI-KACHI YAMA Sazanami
KAI LUNG'S GOLDEN HOURS Bramah
KEEP IT DARK Godber
KEY OUT OF TIME Norton
THE KID FROM MARS Friend
THE KIDNAPPED PRESIDENT Boothby
KILLER BY NIGHT Valdez
KILLER TO COME Merwin
THE KILLING MACHINE Vance
KING HUNTERS Garon
KING OF THE FOURTH PLANET Williams
KING OF THE UNDERSEAS Heming
KING SOLOMON'S MINES Haggard
KINGS OF THE AMAZON Willson
KISS, KISS Dahl
KONGA Owen
THE KRAKEN WAKES Wyndham
THE LABORATORY MEDIUM "Edward"
LABORATORY X Shaw
THE LAD AND THE LION Burroughs
LADDER IN THE SKY Woodcott
LADIES IN HADES Kummer
LADY IN DANGER Williamson
LADY INTO FOX Garnett
THE LADY OF THE SHROUD Stoker
THE LAIR OF THE WHITE WORM Stoker
LAMBDA I AND OTHERS Carnell
LAND BEYOND THE MAP Bulmer
THE LAND OF ESA Charles
LAND OF HIDDEN DEATH Atholl
THE LAND OF HIDDEN MEN Burroughs
LAND OF TERROR Burroughs
THE LAND THAT TIME FORGOT Burroughs
THE LANI PEOPLE Bone
LAST AND FIRST MEN Stapledon
THE LAST ASTRONAUT Torro
THE LAST 14 Barr
THE LAST GENERATION Flecker
THE LAST MARTIAN Statten
THE LAST MUTATION Campbell
THE LAST OF THE AUCAS Aimard
THE LAST PLANET Norton
THE LAST SECRET Chambers
THE LAST SPACE SHIP Leinster
THE LAST VALKYRIE Roberts
LAUGHTER IN SPACE Statten
LEGEND OF LOST EARTH Wallis
THE LEGEND OF SLEEPY HOLLOW Irving
LEGENDS AND TALES Paneth

THE LEGION OF SPACE Williamson
THE LEGION OF THE LIVING DEAD Daly
LEGION OF THE LOST Torro
LEOPARD GOD Garon
LEST DARKNESS FALL de Camp
LEST WE FORGET THEE, EARTH Knox
LET OUT THE BEAST Fischer
LET THE SPACEMEN BEWARE Anderson
LEVEL 7 Roshwald
THE LIE DETECTOR Statten
THE LIFE VAPOR Science Fiction Series #12
LIGHT OF LILITH Wallis
LIGHT OF MARS Charkin
LIGHTNING WORLD Thorpe
THE LIGHTS IN THE SKY ARE STARS Brown
LIMBO Wolfe
LIMEHOUSE NIGHTS Burke
LINE TO TOMORROW Padgett
LISTEN, THE STARS Brunner
LITTLE FUZZY Piper
LLANA OF GATHOL Burroughs
THE LOAFERS OF REFUGE Green
THE LODGER Lowndes
THE LONELY ASTRONOMER Gridban
THE LONELY SHADOWS Merak
LONG AFTERNOON OF EARTH Aldiss
THE LONG LOUD SILENCE Tucker
THE LONG SHIPS Bengtsson
THE LONG TOMORROW Brackett
LOOK BEHIND YOU Burks
LORD KALVAN OF OTHERWHEN Piper
LORD OF THE FLIES Golding
LORD OF THE INCAS Gregory
LORD OF THE SEA Shiel
LORD OF THUNDER Norton
LORDS OF ATLANTIS West
THE LORDS OF MISRULE Pomeroy
LORDS OF THE PSYCHON Galouye
LOST AEONS Cameron
THE LOST CITY Gilson
THE LOST CONTINENT Burroughs
THE LOST GOD Russell
LOST HORIZONS Hilton
THE LOST INCA Inca-Pancho-Ozollo
LOST ISLAND McInnes
THE LOST OASIS Robeson
LOST ON VENUS Burroughs
THE LOST SQUADRON Rochester
THE LOST UNDERWORLD Luigi
LOST WORLD Shaw
THE LOST WORLD Doyle
LOVE IN TIME Harris
THE LOVERS Farmer
THE LOVERS Winsor

LUCINDA Rigsby
THE LUNAR EYE Williams
THE LURKING FEAR Lovecraft

THE MACABRE ONES Fane
THE MACABRE READER Wollheim
THE MACHINE IN WARD 11 Willeford
THE MACHINE THAT THOUGHT Science Fiction Classics #3
THE MAD KING Burroughs
THE MAGIC CHRISTIAN Southern
THE MAGICIAN Maugham
MAGISTER LUDI Hesse
MAGNETIC BRAIN Gridban
MAID OF THURO Lane
THE MAKER OF MOONS Chambers
THE MAKESHIFT ROCKET Anderson
THE MALE RESPONSE Carnell
THE MALIGNANT ENTITY Kline
MAMMALIA Lane
MAMMOTH MAN Sheldon
A MAN CALLED DESTINY Wright
THE MAN FROM BEYOND Muller
THE MAN FROM SPACE Lincoln
THE MAN FROM TOMORROW Statton
THE MAN FROM TOMORROW Tucker
THE MAN IN BLACK Weyman
MAN IN DUPLICATE Statten
A MAN IN THE ZOO Garnett
A MAN OBSESSED Nourse
THE MAN OF BRONZE Robeson
MAN OF EARTH Budrys
MAN OF MANY MINDS Evans
MAN OF TWO WORLDS Jones
MAN OF TWO WORLDS Statten
THE MAN ON THE METEOR Cummings
THE MAN WHO ATE THE WORLD Pohl
THE MAN WHO CAME BACK Thanet
THE MAN WHO CONQUERED TIME Muller
THE MAN WHO COULD STILL LAUGH Houghton
THE MAN WHO COULDN'T DIE Fanthorpe
THE WHO FELL TO EARTH Tevis
THE MAN WHO JAPED Dick
THE MAN WHO LIMPED Kline
THE MAN WHO LIVED FOREVER Miller and Hunger
THE MAN WHO MASTERED TIME Cummings
THE MAN WHO MISSED THE WAR Wheatley
THE MAN WHO SOLD THE MOON Heinlein
THE MAN WHO TILTED THE EARTH Atholl
THE MAN WHO UPSET THE UNIVERSE Asimov
THE MAN WHO WANTED STARS McLaughlin
THE MAN WHO WAS TEN YEARS LATE FOR BREAKFAST Herbert
THE MAN WITH NINE LIVES Ellison
MANKIND ON THE RUN Dickson
THE MARBLE FAUN Hawthorne

MARCH OF THE ROBOTS Brett
THE MARCHING MORONS Kornbluth
MARK OF THE BEAST Muller
MAROONED IN 1492 Cook
MARS IS MY DESTINATION Long
THE MARS MONOPOLY Sohl
THE MARTIAN CHRONICLES Bradbury
MARTIAN MARTYRS Science Fiction Classics #1
THE MARTIAN MISSILE Grinnell
A MARTIAN ODYSSEY Weinbaum
THE MARTIAN SPHINX Woodcott
MARTIAN TIME SLIP Dick
THE MARTIAN WAY Asimov
MARTIANS GO HOME Brown
MARTIANS IN A FROZEN WORLD Conroy
THE MASK OF FU MANCHU Rohmer
THE MASTER MUST DIE Gridban
MASTER OF DREAMS Vincent
THE MASTER OF DWARF ISLAND Whitley
MASTER OF LIFE AND DEATH Silverberg
MASTER OF SPACE Clarke
THE MASTER OF THE DAY OF JUDGMENT Perutz
MASTER OF THE WORLD Verne
MASTER-MIND MENACE Luigi
MASTERMIND OF MARS Burroughs
MASTERS OF EVOLUTION Knight
MASTERS OF THE MAZE Davidson
THE MATING CRY van Vogt
MAYDAY ORBIT Anderson
MAZA OF THE MOON Kline
THE MECHANICAL MAN Science Fiction Series #7
THE MECHANICAL MONARCH Tubb
A MEDICINE FOR MELANCHOLY Bradbury
MEETING AT INFINITY Brunner
MELMOTH THE WANDERER Maturin
THE MEMORY BANK West
MEN AGAINST THE STARS Greenberg
THE MEN FROM THE METEOR Science Fiction Series #13
MEN INTO SPACE Leinster
MEN, MARTIANS AND MACHINES Russell
MEN OF AVALON Keller
MEN ON THE MOON Wollheim
MEN WITHOUT BONES Kersh
THE MENACE FROM EARTH Heinlein
MENACE FROM THE PAST Maddox
THE MENACING SLEEP Sheldon
MESSAGE FROM THE EOCENE St. Clair
A MESSENGER FROM THE UNKNOWN Hawthorne
MESSIAH Vidal
THE METAL EATER Sheldon
THE METAL MONSTER Luigi
THE METAL MONSTER Merritt
METHUSELAH'S CHILDREN Heinlein
METROPOLIS Harbou

MICE OR MACHINES Campbell
MICRO INFINITY Muller
THE MICRO MEN Statten
THE MIDWICH CUCKOOS Wyndham
A MILE BEYOND THE MOON Kornbluth
THE MILE LONG SPACESHIP Wilhelm
THE MILLION CITIES McIntosh
THE MILLION YEAR HUNT Bulmer
THE MIND CAGE van Vogt
MIND FORCE Brett
THE MIND MAKERS Muller
MIND PARTNER Gold
THE MIND SPIDER Leiber
THE MIND THING Brown
MIRANDA Mannon
A MIRROR FOR OBSERVERS Pangborn
MISSION FROM MARS Conroy
MISSION OF GRAVITY Clement
MISSION TO THE STARS Kent
MISSION TO THE STARS van Vogt
MR. ADAM Frank
MR. GEORGE AND OTHER ODD PERSONS Derleth
MR. JONEMACHER'S MACHINE Prime
THE MOLECULE MONSTERS Friend
MOMENT OUT OF TIME Sheldon
MONKEY Wo Cheng-En
MONOGUSA TARO Sazanami
THE MONSTER FROM EARTH'S END Leinster
THE MONSTER MEN Burroughs
THE MONSTER OF THE LAGOON Worts
MONSTERS AND SUCH Leinster
THE MONSTERS OF JUNTONHEIM Hamilton
MOON BASE Tubb
THE MOON CONQUERORS Romans
THE MOON HOAX Locke
THE MOON IS HEAVEN Campbell
THE MOON IS HELL Campbell
THE MOON MAID Burroughs
THE MOON MEN Burroughs
MOON MONSTER Ambrose
THE MOON MONSTERS Marquis
MOON PILOT Buckner
THE MOON POOL Merritt
MOON WAR Hughes
MOONS FOR SALE Gridban
MORE ADVENTURES IN TIME AND SPACE Healy and McComas
MORE ADVENTURES ON OTHER PLANETS Wollheim
MORE FROM ONE STEP BEYOND Bredeson
MORE GHOST STORIES James
MORE MACABRE Wollheim
MORE NOT AT NIGHT Thomson
MORE OF MY FAVORITES IN SUSPENSE Hitchcock
MORE NIGHTMARES Bloch
MORE SOVIET SCIENCE FICTION Asimov

MORE STORIES FROM THE TWILIGHT ZONE Serling
MORE TALES OF TERROR AND SURPRISE Anonymous
MORE THAN HUMAN Sturgeon
MORTALS AND MONSTERS del Rey
THE MORTALS OF RENI Gruen
MOUSE ON THE MOON Wibberley
THE MOUSE THAT ROARED Wibberley
THE MULTIMAN Statten
THE MUMMY COMES TO LIFE Van der Elst
MURDER BY TELECOPTER Hughes
THE MURDER GEM Pollard
MURDER IN SPACE Reed
MURDER IN THE CLINIC Hamilton
THE MURDER OF THE MISSING LINK Vercors
MUTANT Kuttner
THE MUTANT WEAPON Leinster
THE MUTANTS REBEL Tubb
MUTINY IN SPACE Davidson
MY BEST SCIENCE FICTION STORY Margulies and Friend
MY FRIEND THE MURDERER Doyle
MYORA; OR, THE LAND OF ETERNAL SUNSHINE Harvey
THE MYSTERIES OF de Balzac
THE MYSTERIES OF FLORENCE Lippard
THE MYSTERIES OF UDOLPHO Radcliffe
THE MYSTERY OF ARTHUR GORDON PYM Poe and Verne
THE MYSTERY OF DR. FU MANCHU Rohmer
THE MYSTERY OF SATELLITE 7 Coombs
THE MYSTERY OF THE BEETLE Marsh
THE MYSTERY PLANET Kennedy
THE MYSTERY PLANET Roberts
THE MYSTERIOUS ISLAND Verne
THE MYSTERIOUS STRANGER Twain

THE NAKED FOOT Kaner
THE NAKED SUN Asimov
NAKED TO THE STARS Dickson
NATIVES OF SPACE Clement
NAZER Joyce
NEBULA X Statten
THE NECROMANCER Reynolds
NEGATIVE MINUS Fanthorpe
THE NEGATIVE ONES Muller
NEMESIS Fane
THE NEMESIS FROM TERRA Brackett
NERVES del Rey
NEURON WORLD Fanthorpe
A NEW COLLECTION OF GOTHIC STORIES Anonymous Anthology
THE NEW LIFE Science Fiction Classics #4
THE NEW SATELLITE Statten
THE NEW SAXON PAMPHLETS Atkins
NEW STORIES FROM THE TWILIGHT ZONE Serling
NEW TALES OF SPACE AND TIME Healy
NEXT STOP THE STARS Silverberg
THE NEXT WAR Wallace

THE OUTER REACHES Derleth
OUTLAWS OF MARS Kline
OUTSIDE THE UNIVERSE Hamilton
OUTSIDERS: CHILDREN OF WONDER Tenn
OUTPOST MARS Judd
THE OUTWARD URGE Wyndham and Parkes
OVERLORD NEW YORK Elliott
OVERLORDS FROM SPACE Kelleam

PACIFIC ADVANCE Melde
PAGAN PASSIONS Garrett and Harris
A PAIL OF AIR Leiber
PAN SATYRUS Wormser
PARA ROBOT Charles
THE PARADOX MEN Harness
PARASITE PLANET Weinbaum
A PASSAGE TO INDIA Forster
PASSPORT TO ETERNITY Ballard
THE PAWNS OF NULL A van Vogt
PEABODY'S MERMAID Jones
PEBBLE IN THE SKY Asimov
PELLUCIDAR Burroughs
THE PENULTIMATE TRUTH Dick
PEOPLE OF ASA Ashton
THE PEOPLE MAKER Knight
PEOPLE MINUS X Gallun
PEOPLE OF THE TALISMAN Brackett
THE PEOPLE THAT TIME FORGOT Burroughs
PERELANDRA Lewis
THE PERFECT PLANET Smith
PERIL FROM SPACE Maras
PERIL OF CREATION Burton
PERILOUS GALAXY Muller
THE PERMA BOOK OF GHOST STORIES Holland
THE PETRIFIED PLANET Statten
PHANTASIES AND LILITH MacDonald
THE PHANTOM CITY Westall
PHANTOM CRUSADER Brett
PHANTOM OF THE OPERA Leroux
THE PHANTOM ONES Torro
PHANTOMS OF THE DAWN Tweedale
PHOTOMESIS Cameron
THE PICTURE OF DORIAN GRAY Wilde
THE PIGEON Galsworthy
PILGRIMAGE Henderson
PILGRIMAGE TO EARTH Sheckley
"PIONEER 1990" Statten
PIRATES OF CEREBUS Mistral
THE PIRATES OF VENUS Burroughs
THE PIRATES OF ZAN Leinster
PISTOL PAYNE'S JUNGLE SUBNOTANK Belfield
THE PIT AND THE PENDULUM Poe
THE PIXY Reynolds
A PLAGUE OF DEMONS Laumer
PLAGUE SHIP North

PLAN FOR CONQUEST Glynn
PLANET BIG ZERO Hadley
THE PLANET BUYER Smith
THE PLANET EXPLORER Leinster
PLANET FEDERATION Shaw
A PLANET FOR TEXANS Piper
PLANET IN PERIL Christopher
THE PLANET KILLERS Silverberg
PLANET OF NO RETURN Anderson
PLANET OF PERIL Kline
PLANET OF THE APES Boulle
PLANET OF THE DAMNED Harrison
PLANET OF THE DREAMERS MacDonald
THE PLANET OF YOUTH Coblentz
THE PLANET SAVERS Bradley
THE PLANET SEEKERS Barton
THE PLANET STRAPPERS Gallun
PLANET THA Charles
PLANET WAR Fysh
PLANET X Hunt
PLANETARY DISPOSALS, LTD. Gridban
PLANETFALL Hunt
THE PLANETOID PERIL Brown
THE PLOT AGAINST EARTH Knox
THE POCKET BOOK OF ADVENTURE STORIES Stern
THE POCKET BOOK OF GHOST STORIES Stern
THE POCKET BOOK OF MYSTERY STORIES Wright
THE POCKETBOOK OF SCIENCE FICTION Wollheim
PODKAYNE OF MARS Heinlein
POINT COUNTER POINT Huxley
POINT ULTIMATE Sohl
THE POLAR TREASURE Robeson
THE PORT OF PERIL Kline
PORTLAND, OREGON, A. D. 1999 Hayes
PORTRAIT OF A MAN WITH RED HAIR Walpole
POSSIBLE WORLDS OF SCIENCE FICTION Conklin
THE POWER Robinson
POWER SPHERE Brett
A PRANKISH PAIR Davenport
PREFERRED RISK McCann
PRE-GARGANTUA Charles
PRELUDE TO SPACE Clarke
THE PREMATURE BURIAL Poe
PRESIDENT FU MANCHU Rohmer
THE PREVALENCE OF WITCHES Menen
THE PRIMAL URGE Aldiss
THE PRINCE OF PERIL Kline
A PRINCESS OF MARS Burroughs
THE PRINCESS OF THE ATOM Cummings
THE PRIVATE LIFE OF HELEN OF TROY Erskine
PRIVATE MEMOIRS AND CONFESSIONS OF A JUSTIFIED SINNER Hogg
THE PRODIGAL SUN High
PROJECTILE WAR Lang
PROJECTION INFINITY Zeigfried
THE PSIONIC MENACE Woodcott

THE PURCHASE OF THE NORTH POLE Verne
THE PUPPET MASTERS Heinlein
PURPLE ISLANDS Carter
THE PURPLE SAPPHIRE Taine
THE PURPLE WIZARD Gridban
THE PUZZLE PLANET Lowndes
QUATERMASS AND THE PIT Kneale
THE QUATERMASS EXPERIMENT Kneale
QUATERMASS II Kneale
QUEEN OF THE SKIES Bidston
THE QUEEN PEOPLE Rey
QUEER LOOKING BOX Hervey
QUEST OF THE DAWN MAN Rosny

RACE TO THE STARS Margulies and Friend
RADAR ALERT Zeigfried
THE RADIO BEASTS Farley
THE RADIO PLANET Farley
THE RADIUM KING Burton
RAIDERS FROM THE RINGS Nourse
THE RAIDERS OF ROBOT CITY Roberts
RALPH 124C 41 Gernsback
THE RAT RACE Franklin
REACH FOR TOMORROW Clarke
REACTOR XK9 Muller
THE REBELLERS Roberts
THE REBELLIOS STARS Asimov
REBELS OF THE RED PLANET Fontenay
REBIRTH McClary
RE-BIRTH Wyndham
RECALLED TO LIFE Silverberg
RECRUIT FOR ANDROMEDA Lesser
RED ALERT Bryant
THE RED BRAIN Hammett
RED DEATH OF MARS Williams
THE RED HAIRED GIRL Herbert
THE RED INSECTS Statten
RED MEN OF MARS Fearn
THE RED PLANET Campbell
THE RED PLANET Winterbotham
RED SNOW Moxley
RED STORM Storm
THE REEFS OF SPACE Pohl and Williamson
RE-ENTER FU MANCHU Rohmer
REGAN'S PLANET Silverberg
THE REIGN OF WIZARDRY Williamson
RENDEZVOUS ON A LOST WORLD Chandler
THE RENEGADE STAR Statten
THE REPAIRMEN OF CYCLOPS Brunner
REPLY PAID Heard
REPTILICUS Owen
THE REPUBLIC OF THE FUTURE Dodd
RESEARCH OPTA Charles
REST IN AGONY Jorgensen

THE REST MUST DIE Foster
RESURGENT DUST Garner
THE RESURRECTED MAN Tubb
THE RETURN de la Mare
THE RETURN Torro
THE RETURN OF FU MANCHU Rohmer
THE RETURN OF KARL MARX Lynn
RETURN OF SUMURU Rohmer
THE RETURN OF TARZAN Burroughs
THE RETURN OF THE HERO Figgis
THE RETURN OF THE KING Tolkien
THE RETURN OF ZEUS Muller
RETURN TO EARTH Berry
RETURN TO OTHERNESS Kuttner
RETURN TO TOMORROW Hubbard
REVERSE UNIVERSE Gridban
REVOLT IN 2100 Heinlein
THE REVOLT OF THE ANGELS France
REVOLT OF THE TRIFFIDS Wyndham
THE RIDDLE OF THE SANDS Childers
RIDERS TO THE STARS Siodmak
THE RIM OF SPACE Chandler
RING AROUND THE SUN Simak
RINGSTONES Sarban
THE RISE AND FALL OF THE UNITED STATES A Diplomat
THE RITES OF ONE Brunner
THE RITHIAN TERROR Knight
THE RIVAL ROBOTS Roberts
R. L. S. FABULOUS RACONTEUR Stevenson
ROAR OF THE ROCKET Friend
THE ROBOT JU-JU Dane
THE ROBOT MAN Allingham
ROBOTS AND CHANGELINGS del Rey
ROCKET INVASION Lang
ROCKET TO LIMBO Nourse
ROCKET TO THE MORGUE Boucher
THE ROCKETEERS Roberts
RODENT MUTATION Fane
ROGUE IN SPACE Brown
ROGUE MOON Budrys
ROGUE QUEEN de Camp
ROMANCE IN BLACK Field
ROOKWOOD, A ROMANCE Ainsworth
THE ROOM IN THE DRAGON INN Le Fanu
A ROUND TRIP TO THE YEAR 2000 Cook
THE RULE OF THE PAGBEASTS McIntosh
THE RUNNING MAN Holly
A RUSSIAN PRINCESS Turnerelli
RITHA RIDES THE ROCKET Science Fiction Classics #6
ST. ANDREW'S GHOST STORIES Linskill
THE SAINT'S CHOICE OF IMPOSSIBLE CRIMES Charteris
A SAKI SAMPLER Munro
SALAMBO Flaubert
SALOME Viereck and Eldridge
SANCTUARY IN THE SKY Brunner

SANDS OF ETERNITY Fanthorpe
SANDS OF MARS Clarke
THE SARAGOSSA MANUSCRIPT Potocki
SARDONICUS Russell
SARGASSO OF SPACE North
THE SATANIC POWER Van der Elst
THE SATANIST Wheatley
SATELLITE B. C. Le Page
SATELLITE E ONE Castle
THE SATURDAY EVENING POST FANTASY READER Fles
SATURN PATROL Lang
SAVAGE PELLUCIDAR Burroughs
THE SCARF OF PASSION Bloch
SCAVENGERS IN SPACE Nourse
SCIENCE FICTION ADVENTURES IN DIMENSION Conklin
SCIENCE FICTION ADVENTURES IN MUTATION Conklin
SCIENCE FICTION CARNIVAL Brown and Reynolds
THE SCIENCE FICTION GALAXY Conklin
SCIENCE FICTION OMNIBUS Conklin
SCIENCE FICTION TERROR TALES Conklin
SCIENCE FICTION THINKING MACHINES Conklin
SCIENCE METROPOLIS Statten
SCOURGE OF THE ATOM Gridban
SEA KISSED Bloch
SEA SIEGE Norton
THE SEA SPIDER Rochester
THE SEARCH FOR ZEI de Camp
SEARCH THE DARK STARS Muller
SEARCH THE SKY Pohl and Kornbluth
THE SECOND ATLANTIS Williams
SECOND ENDING White
2nd FOUNDATION: GALACTIC EMPIRE Asimov
THE SECOND GHOST BOOK Asquith
THE SECOND PAN BOOK OF HORROR STORIES van Thal
SECONDS Ely
SECRET AGENT OF TERRA Brunner
THE SECRET KINGDOM Roberts
THE SECRET MARTIANS Sharkey
THE SECRET MASTERS Kersh
SECRET OF SINHARET Brackett
SECRET OF THE LOST RACE Norton
SECRET OF THE MARTIAN MOONS Wollheim
THE SECRET OF THE STRADIVARIUS Conway
THE SECRET OF ZI Bulmer
THE SECRET POWER Van der Elst
THE SECRET VISITORS White
THE SECRET WAR Wheatley
THE SEED OF EARTH Silverberg
SEED OF LIGHT Cooper
THE SEEDLING STARS Blish
SEEDS OF LIFE Taine
THE SEEDS OF TIME Wyndham
SELECTED GREAT STORIES Hecht
SELECTED TALES OF ALGERNON BLACKWOOD Blackwood
SENTINELS OF SPACE Russell

SERGEANT TERRY BULL Bull
SEVEN FOOTPRINTS TO SATAN Merritt
SEVEN FROM THE STARS Bradley
SEVEN MASTERPIECES OF GOTHIC HORROR Spector
SEVEN MORE STRANGE STORIES Hardie
SEVEN STRANGE STORIES Hardie
17 X INFINITY Conklin
7th ANNUAL YEAR'S BEST S F Merril
THE SEVENTH DAY Kirst
THE 7th DIMENSION La Salle
THE SEX WAR Merwin
S F: THE YEAR'S GREATEST Merril
S F: YEAR'S GREATEST 2nd VOLUME Merril
S F: YEAR'S GREATEST 3rd VOLUME Merril
S F: YEAR'S GREATEST 4th VOLUME Merril
THE SHADOW GIRL Cummings
SHADOW OF FU MANCHU Rohmer
SHADOW OF TOMORROW Pohl
THE SHADOW ON THE SEA Pemberton
SHADOW OVER MARS Brackett
SHADOWS IN THE SUN Oliver
SHADOWS WITH EYES Leiber
SHAMBLEAU Moore
SHANADU Briney
THE SHAPE OF THINGS Knight
SHARDS OF SPACE Sheckley
SHE Haggard
SHIELD Anderson
SHIP ASHORE Parkman
THE SHIP FROM NOWHERE Science Fiction Series #18
THE SHIP FROM OUTSIDE Chandler
THE SHIP OF ISHTER Merritt
THE SHIP THAT SAILED THE TIME STREAM Edmondson
SHIPS OF VERO Shaw
SHIPS TO THE STARS Leiber
SHOCK Matheson
SHOCK II Matheson
THE SHORES OF SPACE Matheson
THE SHORT REIGN OF PIPPIN IV Steinbeck
SHOT IN THE DARK Merril
THE SHRINKING MAN Matheson
THE SHROUDED ABBOT Fanthorpe
SHUDDERING CASTLE Fawley
SHUNA AND THE LOST TRIBE King
SHUNA, WHITE QUEEN OF THE JUNGLE King
SIEGE OF THE UNSEEN van Vogt
SIGN OF THE LABRYS St. Clair
THE SILENT CITY Thorpe
THE SILENT INVADERS Silverberg
SILENT RIVER Garon
THE SILVER EGGHEADS Leiber
THE SIMULACRA Dick
SIN IN SPACE Judd
SINISTER BARRIER Russell

SINISTER MADONNA Rohmer
THE SIOUX SPACEMAN Norton
THE SIRENS OF TITAN Vonnegut
SISTER EARTH Brede
6 AND THE SILENT SCREAM Howard
6 FROM WORLDS BEYOND Dikty
SIX GREAT SHORT NOVELS OF SCIENCE FICTION Conklin
SIX WORLDS YONDER Russell
6 X H Heinlein
6th ANNUAL YEAR'S BEST S F Merril
SIXTY DAYS TO LIVE Wheatley
SKIN AND BONES Smith
THE SKULL OF KANAIMA Norwood
THE SKY BLOCK Frazee
THE SKYLARK OF SPACE Smith
THE SKYLARK OF VALERON Smith
SKYLARK THREE Smith
THE SKYNAPPERS Brunner
SKYPORT Siodmak
SLAN van Vogt
SLAVE PLANET Janifer
SLAVE SHIP Pohl
SLAVE TRADERS OF THE SKY Future
SLAVERS OF SPACE Brunner
SLAVES OF IJAX Fearn
SLAVES OF SUMURU Rohmer
SLAVES OF THE KLAU Vance
SLEEP IS DEATH Kensch
THE SMUGGLED ATOM BOMB Wylie
THE SNAKE LADY Lee
SNAKE VALLEY Garon
THE SNAKE'S PASS Stoker
SNOW FURY Holden
SNOWFLAKES IN THE SUN Ganley
THE SNOWS OF GANYMEDE Anderson
SOFTLY BY MOONLIGHT Fane
SOJARR OF TITAN Wellman
SOLAR GRAVITA Cameron
SOLAR LOTTERY Dick
THE SOLDADO ANT Jenkins
SOLUTION T-25 DuBois
SOME OF YOUR BLOOD Sturgeon
SOMEONE LIKE YOU Dahl
SOMETHING ABOUT SPIDERS Merak
SOMETHING WICKED THIS WAY COMES Bradbury
SOMETIME NEVER Golding, Wyndham, Peake
SOMEWHERE OUT THERE Fane
SON OF ABDAN Webster
THE SON OF TARZAN Burroughs
SON OF THE TREE Vance
THE SOUND OF HIS HORN Sarban
SOVIET SCIENCE FICTION Asimov
THE SPACE BARBARIANS Godwin
SPACE BEAM Robb

SPACE-BORNE Fanthorpe
THE SPACE BORN Tubb
SPACE BY THE TAIL Bixby
THE SPACE EGG Winterbotham
SPACE FLIGHT Hunt
SPACE FLIGHT 139 Mistral
THE SPACE FRONTIERS Vernon
SPACE FURY Fanthorpe
SPACE HUNGER Grey
SPACE LINE Lang
SPACE LORDS Smith
SPACE MEN Shaw
THE SPACE MERCHANTS Pohl and Kornbluth
SPACE NO BARRIER Torro
SPACE ON MY HANDS Brown
SPACE OPERA Vance
THE SPACE PIRATE Vance
SPACE PIRATES del Martia
SPACE PLAGUE Smith
SPACE PLATFORM Leinster
SPACE PRISON Godwin
SPACE SALVAGE Bulmer
SPACE STATION #1 Long
THE SPACE-TIME JUGGLER Brunner
SPACE TRAP Bell
SPACE TREASON Clarke and Bulmer
SPACE TUG Leinster
SPACE VIKING Piper
SPACE VOID Muller
THE SPACE WARP Statten
THE SPACE WILLIES Russell
SPACEHIVE Sutton
SPACIAL DELIVERY Dickson
SPACEWARD HO! Molesworth
SPACEWAYS Maine
THE SPANISH CAVE Household
SPATIAL RAY Hunt
SPAWN OF SPACE Harkon
SPAWN OF THE VAMPIRE Firth
SPECIAL MISSION Muller
THE SPECTRAL BRIDE Shearing
THE SPECTRE BULLET Science Fiction Series #17
SPECTRE OF DARKNESS Muller
SPECTRUM Amis and Conquest
SPECTRUM II Amis and Conquest
THE SPELL OF SEVEN de Camp
SPHERO NOVA Cameron
THE SPHINX CHILD Mullen
THE SPOT OF LIFE Hall
SPRAGUE DE CAMP'S NEW ANTHOLOGY de Camp
SQUARING THE TRIANGLE Kaner
THE SQUID Horan
THE STAINLESS STEEL RAT Harrison
STAR BORN Norton
STAR BRIDGE Williamson and Gunn

THE STAR DWELLERS Blish
STAR GATE Norton
STAR GUARD Norton
STAR HUNTER Norton
THE STAR KING Vance
THE STAR MAKER Stapledon
THE STAR OF LIFE Hamilton
STAR OF STARS Pohl
STAR SCIENCE FICTION STORIES Pohl
STAR SCIENCE FICTION STORIES No. 2 Pohl
STAR SCIENCE FICTION STORIES No. 3 Pohl
STAR SCIENCE FICTION STORIES No. 4 Pohl
STAR SCIENCE FICTION STORIES No. 5 Pohl
STAR SCIENCE FICTION STORIES No. 6 Pohl
THE STAR SEEKER Rayer
STAR SHINE Brown
STAR SHORT NOVELS Pohl
STAR SURGEON White
THE STAR WASPS Williams
STAR WAYS Anderson
STARBURST Bester
STARHAVEN Jorgenson
THE STARS ARE OURS Bulmer
THE STARS ARE OURS Norton
THE STARS ARE TOO HIGH Behnson
THE STARS LIKE DUST Asimov
THE STARS MY DESTINATION Bester
STARSHIP Aldiss
STARSHIP TROOPERS Heinlein
STARSWARM Aldiss
STATION IN SPACE Gunn
STATION 7 Hunt
THE STATUS CIVILIZATION Sheckley
STELLA RADIUM DISCHARGE Luna
THE STELLAR LEGION Tubb
STEPPENWOLF Hesse
STEPSONS OF TERRA Silverberg
STILL NOT AT NIGHT Thomson
A STIR OF ECHOES Matheson
THE STONE OF CHASTITY Sharp
STORE OF INFINITY Sheckley
STORIES Bowen
STORIES FROM THE DIARY OF A DOCTOR: 2nd SERIES Meade and Halifax
STORIES FROM THE TWILIGHT ZONE Serling
STORIES OF FEAR McLaren
STORIES OF SCIENTIFIC IMAGINATION Gallant
STORIES OF THE SUPERNATURAL Sayers
STORIES UNEXPECTED Cerf
STORIES WITH A VENGEANCE Sala
STORM GOD'S FURY Fane
STORM OVER WARLOCK Norton
STOWAWAY TO MARS Beynon
THE STORY OF MY DICTATORSHIP Anonymous
THE STRANGE CASE OF DR. JEKYLL AND MR. HYDE Stevenson

THE STRANGE CASE OF MISS ANNIE SPRAGGE Bromfield
A STRANGE CONFLICT Batchellor
STRANGE CONFLICT Wheatley
THE STRANGE DOCTOR Van der Elst
STRANGE HUNGER Hervey
STRANGE LOVE STORIES Anonymous
STRANGE OFFSPRING Palmer
THE STRANGE ONES Torro
A STRANGE PEOPLE Batchellor
STRANGE PORTS OF CALL Derleth
STRANGE RELATIONS Farmer
STRANGE ROMANCE Herbert
STRANGE STORIES, THE LAST SEVEN Hardie
STRANGE TALES Anonymous
THE STRANGE VISITATION OF JOSIAH MCNASON Corelli
THE STRANGE WORLD OF ARTHUR MACHEN Machen
STRANGER THAN YOU THINK Edmondson
STRANGERS FROM EARTH Anderson
STRANGERS IN THE UNIVERSE Simak
THE STRATOSPHERE PATROL Molesworth
THE STRAY LAMB Smith
THE STRIKE OF A SEX Miller
STURGEON IN ORBIT Sturgeon
SUCH POWER IS DANGEROUS Wheatley
SUGGESTION Collins
THE SUN MAKERS Statten
THE SUN SABOTEURS Knight
THE SUN SMASHER Hamilton
THE SUNDIAL Jackson
THE SUNKEN WORLD Coblentz
SUNS IN DUO La Salle
THE SUPER BARBARIANS Brunner
SUPERMIND Phillips
THE SUPERNATURAL READER Conklin
THE SURVIVOR Lovecraft and Derleth
SUSPENSE STORIES Hitchcock
SUSPENSION Fane
SWORD OF ALDONES Bradley
SWORD OF RHIANNON Brackett
SWORDS OF MARS Burroughs
SWORDS AND SORCERY de Camp
THE SWORDSMAN OF MARS Kline
SWORDSMEN IN THE SKY Wollheim
THE SYNDIC Kornbluth
THE SYNTHETIC MAN Sturgeon
SYNTHETIC MEN OF MARS Burroughs
THE SYNTHETIC ONES Roberts

TAKEOFF Kornbluth
TALENTS, INCORPORATED Leinster
TALES FROM THE ARABIAN NIGHTS Burton
TALES FROM GEHENNA Nobel
TALES FROM THE DECAMERON Boccaccio
TALES FROM THE WHITE HART Clarke

TALES IN A JUGULAR VEIN Bloch
· TALES OF CHINATOWN Rohmer
TALES OF DETECTION AND MYSTERY Sayers
TALES OF GOOSEFLESH AND LAUGHTER Wyndham
TALES OF LOVE AND HORROR Congdon
TALES OF MURDER AND MYSTERY Anonymous
TALES OF MYSTERY AND SURPRISE Anonymous
TALES OF OUTER SPACE Wollheim
TALES OF PIRACE, CRIME AND GHOSTS DeFoe
TALES OF TEN WORLDS Clarke
TALES OF TERROR Anonymous
TALES OF TERROR Poe
TALES OF TERROR AND THE UNKNOWN Anonymous
TALES OF THE SUPERNATURAL Anonymous
TALES OF THE UNCANNY Anonymous
TALES OF THE WEIRD St. Germain
TALES TO BE TOLD IN THE DARK Davenport
TALL SHORT STORIES Duthie
TAMA-NO-I Sazanami
TANAR OF PELLUCIDAR Burroughs
TARNISHED UTOPIA Jameson
TARZAN AND THE ABOMINABLE SNOWMAN Werper
TARZAN AND THE ANT MEN Burroughs
TARZAN AND THE CASTAWAYS Burroughs
TARZAN·AND THE CAVE CITY Werper
TARZAN AND THE CITY OF GOLD Burroughs
TARZAN AND THE FORBIDDEN CITY Burroughs
TARZAN AND THE FOREIGN LEGION Burroughs
TARZAN AND THE GOLDEN LION Burroughs
TARZAN AND THE JEWELS OF OPAR Burroughs
TARZAN AND THE LEOPARD MAN Burroughs
TARZAN AND THE LION MAN Burroughs
TARZAN AND THE LOST EMPIRE Burroughs
TARZAN AND THE MADMAN Burroughs
TARZAN AND THE SILVER GLOBE Werper
TARZAN AND THE SNAKE PEOPLE Werper
TARZAN AND THE WINGED INVADERS Werper
TARZAN AT THE EARTH'S CORE Burroughs
TARZAN, LORD OF THE JUNGLE Burroughs
TARZAN OF THE APES Burroughs
TARZAN THE INVINCIBLE Burroughs
TARZAN THE MAGNIFICENT Burroughs
TARZAN THE TERRIBLE Burroughs
TARZAN THE UNTAMED Burroughs
TARZAN TRIUMPHANT Burroughs
TARZAN'S QUEST Burroughs
TASK FLIGHT Lang
A TASTE FOR HONEY Heard
TAWARA TODA HIDESATO Sazanami
TELEPATH Sellings
THE TELEVISION DETECTIVE Keller
THE TEMPLE OF THE DEAD Norwood
TEN FROM INFINITY Jorgenson
TEN YEARS TO DOOMSDAY Anderson and Kurland

TERMINAL BEACH Ballard
TERRA! Lang
TERROR ABOVE THE STRATOSPHERE Kinson
TERROR AT NIGHT Williams
TERROR FROM THE STRATOSPHERE Maxwell
THE TERROR FROM TIMORKAL Pragnell
TERROR OF THE LEOPARD MEN Kennerley
TERROR STRIKES Firth
TERROR-TRAP Lazenby
THARKOL, LORD OF THE UNKNOWN Hamilton
THAT HIDEOUS STRENGTH Léwis
THERE WERE NO ASPER LADIES Ascher
THEY CAME FROM MARS Cockcroft
THEY FOUND ATLANTIS Wheatley
THEY NEVER COME BACK Brett
THEY WALKED LIKE MEN Simak
THIEVES OF THE AIR Herbert and Pragnell
A THIN GHOST James
THE THING Campbell
A THING OF THE PAST Gridban
THE THING THAT MADE LOVE Reed
THINGS Howard
THINGS WITH CLAWS Burnett
THE THINKING MACHINE Futrelle
THIRD FROM THE SUN Matheson
THE THIRD GALAXY READER Gold
THE THIRD LEVEL Finney
13 GREAT STORIES OF SCIENCE FICTION Conklin
13 MORE STORIES THEY WOULDN'T LET ME DO ON T V Hitchcock
THE 13th IMMORTAL Silverberg
30 DAY WONDER Wilson
THIRTY MILES DOWN Science Fiction Series #12
THIS FORTRESS WORLD Gunn
THIS PLANET FOR SALE Hay
THIS WEEK'S STORIES OF MYSTERY AND SUSPENSE Beach
THIS WORLD IS TABOO Leinster
THOSE IDIOTS FROM EARTH Wilson
THE THOUGHT PROJECTOR Science Fiction Series #2
THE THOUGHT READER Sanforde
THE THOUGHT STEALER Science Fiction Series #7
THE THOUGHT TRANSLATOR Science Fiction Series #9
THE THOUSAND HEADED MAN Robeson
A 1000 YEARS ON Muller
THREE AGAINST THE WITCH WORLD Norton
THE THREE ETERNALS Binder
THREE FACES OF TIME Merwin
3 FROM OUT THERE Margulies
THREE GO BACK Mitchell
THREE HEARTS AND THREE LIONS Anderson
THREE IN ONE Sturgeon, Simak, Leinster
THE THREE ROCKETEERS Molesworth
THE THREE SUNS OF ANARA Temple
3 THOUSAND YEARS McClary
3 TIMES INFINITY Margulies
THREE TO CONQUER Russell

THREE WORLDS OF FUTURITY St. Clair
THREE WORLDS TO CONQUER Anderson
THRESHOLD OF ETERNITY Brunner
THRILLING STORIES - ROMANCE, ADVENTURE Anonymous
THROUGH THE BARRIER Torro
THROUGH THE FORBIDDEN GATES Anonymous
THUNDER ON THE LEFT Morley
THUVIA, MAID OF MARS Burroughs
THE TIDE WENT OUT Maine
TIGER BY THE TAIL Nourse
TIGER GIRL Hamilton
TILL WE HAVE FACES Lewis
TIME AND AGAIN Simak
TIME AND SPACE Le Page
TIME AND STARS Anderson
A TIME APPOINTED Statten
THE TIME BRIDGE Statten
THE TIME DISSOLVER Sohl
TIME HAS A DOOR Kensch
TIME IN ADVANCE Tenn
TIME IS THE SIMPLEST THING Simak
THE TIME MACHINE Wells
THE TIME MASTERS Tucker
TIME MUST HAVE A STOP Huxley
TIME OUT FOR TOMORROW Wilson
THE TIME STREAM Taine
THE TIME THIEF Valdez
TIME TO COME Derleth
TIME TO TELEPORT Dickson
THE TIME TRADERS Norton
TIME TRAP Phillips
THE TIME TRAP Statten
TIME TUNNEL Leinster
THE TIME TWISTERS Holly
TIME X Tucker
TIMELESS STORIES Bradbury
TIMELINER Maine
TIMES WITHOUT NUMBER Brunner
TITAN'S DAUGHTER Blish
TITAN'S MOON Charles
TO CONQUER CHAOS Brunner
TO LIVE FOREVER Vance
TO THE DEVIL - A DAUGHTER Wheatley
TO THE END OF TIME Williams
TO THE SUN Verne
TO THE TOMBAUGH STATION Tucker
TO THE ULTIMATE Statten
TO WALK THE NIGHT Sloane
TOLD IN THE DARK, A BOOK OF UNCANNY STORIES van Thal
TOLD IN THE DARK, NINE UNCANNY STORIES van Thal
TOMORROW Wylie
TOMORROW AND TOMORROW Collins
THE TOMORROW PEOPLE Merril
TOMORROW PLUS X Tucker

TOMORROW THE STARS Heinlein
TOMORROW X 4 Knight
TOMORROW TIMES SEVEN Pohl
TOMORROW'S GIFT Cooper
TOMORROW'S UNIVERSE Campbell
TONGUES OF THE MOON Farmer
TOPPER Smith
TOPPER TAKES A TRIP Smith
THE TORCH OF RA Science Fiction Series #8
TORMENTED CITY Grey
THE TORTURED PLANET Lewis
A TOUCH OF INFINITY Ellison
A TOUCH OF STRANGE Sturgeon
TOWER OF ZANID de Camp
THE TOWERS OF TORON Delany
A TRACE OF MEMORY Laumer
THE TRAIL OF FU MANCHU Rohmer
THE TRAIL OF THE SERPENT Southworth
THE TRANSCENDENT MAN Sohl
TRANSFINITE MAN Kapp
TRANS-MERCURIAN Lang
TRANSIT Cooper
THE TRANSPOSED MAN Swain
TRAPS Duerrenmatt
THE TREASURE OF THE GOLDEN CRATER Lounsberry
A TREASURY OF SCIENCE FICTION Conklin
THE TREMBLING WORLD del Martia
TREMOR Lederman
THE TRIAL OF TERRA Williamson
TRIBAL WAR Garon
A TRIP TO MARS Cobb
TRI-PLANET Kellar
THE TRIPLE MAN Fanthorpe
THE TRIUMPH OF TIME Blish
TROUBLE WITH LICHEN Wyndham
TROUBLE WITH TYCHO Simak
TROUBLED STAR Smith
TUNNEL FROM CALAIS Rame
TURN LEFT AT THURSDAY Pohl
THE TURN OF THE SCREW James
TURNABOUT Smith
12 STORIES FOR LATE AT NIGHT Hitchcock
12 STORIES THEY WOULDN'T LET ME DO ON T V Hitchcock
12 TO THE MOON Wise
21st CENTURY SUB Herbert
THE TWENTY-SECOND CENTURY Christopher
TWENTY-FOUR HOURS Charles
25 GREAT GHOST STORIES Anonymous
THE 27th DAY Mantley
29,000 LEAGUES UNDER THE SEA Verne
TWICE IN TIME Wellman
TWICE TOLD TALES Hawthorne
TWICE UPON A STAR Fontenay
TWILIGHT ANCESTORS Fanthorpe

TWILIGHT OF REASON Burke
THE TWISTED MEN van Vogt
TWISTS IN TIME Leinster
TWO DAYS OF TERROR Sheldon
TWO FAMOUS STORIES: JUSTICE and THE RAT Wright
200 YEARS TO CHRISTMAS McIntosh
TWO HUNDRED MILLION A. D. van Vogt
2000 YEARS ON Statten
THE TWO TOWERS Tolkien
TWO WORLDS Lorraine
TYPEWRITER IN THE SKY and FEAR Hubbard

THE ULTIMATE INVADER Russell
THE ULTIMATE MAN Muller
ULTIMATUM IN 2050 A. D. Sharkey
ULTRA SPECTRUM Statten
UNCANNY Bachelor
UNCANNY ADVENTURES Ascher
UNCANNY TALES Hopkins
UNCHARTED SEAS Wheatley
UNCLE SAM'S CABINS Davenport
UNDER THE INFLUENCE Kerr
UNDERWORLD OF ZELLO Deegan
THE UNDYING FIRE Pratt
UNEARTHLY NEIGHBORS Oliver
THE UNEXPECTED Margulies
UNEXPECTED DIMENSION Budrys
THE UNFORSEEN Macardle
UNHOLY FLAME Rosmanith
THE UNINVITED Macardle
THE UNINVITED Muller
UNIVERSE Heinlein
THE UNIVERSE AGAINST HER Schmitz
THE UNIVERSE MAKER van Vogt
THE UNKNOWN Bensen
UNKNOWN DESTINY Fane
THE UNKNOWN FIVE Bensen
UN-MAN AND OTHER STORIES Anderson
THE UNPOSSESSED Muller
THE UNQUIET CORPSE Sloane
THE UNSEEN Barton
THE UNSLEEP Gillon
THE UNTAMED Norwood
UNTOUCHED BY HUMAN HANDS Sheckley
URANIA Flammarion
THE URANIUM SEEKERS Zeigfried
URANIUM 235 Muller
UTOPIA 14 Vonnegut

VALLEY OF CREATION Kuttner
VALLEY OF PRETENDERS Science Fiction Classics #2
VALLEY OF TERROR Rey
VALLEY OF THE FLAME Kuttner
THE VALLEY OF THE GREAT RAY Science Fiction Series #11

THE VAMPIRE Fox
VAMPIRES OF VENUS Mannheim
VANDOVER AND THE BRUTE Norris
VANGUARD FROM ALPHA Aldiss
THE VANGUARD OF VENUS Bartlett
VANGUARD TO NEPTUNE Walsh
THE VARIABLE MAN Dick
VEGA Hunt
VENGEANCE OF SIVA Muller
THE VENOM SEEKERS Berry
VENUS PLUS X Sturgeon
THE VENUS VENTURE Muller
VENUSIAN ADVENTURE Tubb
THE VICTORIAN CHAISE LOUNGE Laski
THE VIEW FROM THE STARS Miller
VILLAGE OF STARS Stanton
VILLAGE OF THE DAMNED Wyndham
VIRGIN PLANET Anderson
VIRUS X Horler
VISION OF THE DAMNED Fanthorpe
VISIT TO A SMALL PLANET Vidal
THE VOICE COMMANDS Science Fiction Classics #5
THE VOICES OF TIME Ballard
THE VOID BEYOND Williams
VOODOO PLANET North
VOR Blish
VOYAGE INTO SPACE van Loden
THE VOYAGE OF THE SPACE BEAGLE van Vogt
VOYAGE TO THE BOTTOM OF THE SEA Sturgeon
VOYAGE TO VENUS Lewis
VULCAN'S HAMMER Dick
VULL THE INVISIBLE Murdock
WAGNER, THE WEHR-WOLF Reynolds
THE WAILING ASTEROID Leinster
WALDO AND MAGIC, INC. Heinlein
WALDO: GENIUS IN ORBIT Heinlein
WALK THROUGH TOMORROW Zeigfried
THE WALKER THROUGH WALLS Ayme
THE WALL Grey
WALL AROUND THE WORLD Cogswell
THE WALTZ OF DEATH Maxon
THE WANDERER Leiber
WANDERER OF SPACE Statten
THE WANDERING SPIRIT; OR, MEMOIRS OF THE HOUSE OF MORNE Anonymous
WANDL, THE INVADER Cummings
THE WAR AGAINST THE RULL van Vogt
THE WAR CHIEF Burroughs
WAR OF ARGUS LePage
WAR LORDS OF SPACE Hughes
THE WAR OF THE WORLDS Wells
WAR OF THE WING MEN Anderson
THE WAR OF TWO WORLDS Anderson
WAR WITH THE GIZMOS Leinster
WAR WITH THE NEWTS Capek

WAR WITH THE ROBOTS Harrison
WARRIOR OF LLARN Fox
WARRIOR OF MARS Fearn
THE WARRIORS OF DAY Blish
WARLORD OF KOR Carr
THE WARLORD OF MARS Burroughs
WASP Russell
THE WATER DEVIL Marriott
WATERS OF LETHE Keller
A WAY HOME Sturgeon
WAY OUT Howard
WAY STATION Simak
WE Zamiatin
WE CAST NO SHADOW Rayer
WE CLAIM THESE STARS Anderson
WE WHO SURVIVED Nool
WEALTH OF THE VOID Statten
THE WEAPON SHOPS OF ISHER van Vogt
WEB OF THE WITCH WORLD Norton
WEIRD AND UNCANNY STORIES Hopkins
WEIRD AND OCCULT MISCELLANY Anonymous
A WEIRD GIFT Ohnet
THE WEIRD HOUSE Heming
THE WEIRD MAN Roberts
THE WEIRD ONES Gold
THE WEIRD SHADOW OVER INNSMOUTH Lovecraft
WEIRD TALES Margulies
WELL OF THE WORLDS Padgett
WEREWOLF AT LARGE Fanthorpe
THE WEREWOLF OF PARIS Endore
WHAT MAD UNIVERSE? Brown
WHAT MAY HAPPEN IN THE NEXT 90 DAYS Anonymous
WHAT STRANGE STARS AND SKIES Davidson
WHEN AGE GROWS YOUNG Kirk
WHEN THE EARTH DIED Mannheim
WHEN THE GODS CAME Adams
WHEN THE GREAT APES CAME Martin
WHEN THE KISSING HAD TO STOP Fitzgibbon
WHEN THE MOON FELL Science Fiction Series #6
WHEN THE SLEEPER WAKES Wells
WHEN THE SUN WENT OUT Science Fiction Series #4
WHEN THE WORLD CRASHED Belfield
WHEN THEY COME FROM SPACE Clifton
WHEN TIME STOOD STILL Orkow
WHEN WORLDS COLLIDE Balmer and Wylie
WHERE ETERNITY ENDS Binder
WHERE THEY BREED Royer
THE WHISPERING GORILLA Reed
WHITE AUGUST Boland
THE WHITE WOLF Gregory
THE WHITE SIBYL Smith
WHITE VOYAGE Christopher
WHO? Budrys
WHO FEARS THE DEVIL? Wellman

WHO GOES THERE? Campbell
WHO SPEAKS OF CONQUEST Wright
THE WHOLE MAN Brunner
WHOM THE GODS DESTROY Bennett
WIELAND, OR THE TRANSFORMATION Brown
WILD ADVENTURES ROUND THE POLE Stables
THE WIND BENDERS Kennaway
THE WIND FROM NOWHERE Ballard
THE WINDS OF TIME Oliver
WINDSOR CASTLE Ainsworth
WINGS ACROSS TIME Arnold
WINTERS TALES Dinesen
WITCH HOUSE Walton
WITCH WORLD Norton
WITCHES, WARLOCKS AND WEREWOLVES Serling
THE WITCHING NIGHT Cody
THE WIZARD OF LEMURIA Carter
THE WIZARD OF LINN van Vogt
THE WIZARD OF OZ Baum
WIZARD OF STARSHIP POSEIDON Bulmer
WOLFBANE Pohl and Kornbluth
A WOMAN A DAY Farmer
WOMAN DOMINANT Vivian
THE WONDER EFFECT Pohl and Kornbluth
THE WONDER WAR Janifer
WORLD AFLAME Bulmer
WORLD AT BAY Tubb
THE WORLD BELOW Wright
THE WORLD GRABBERS Fairman
WORLD IN A TEST TUBE Campbell
THE WORLD IN DARKNESS Roberts
THE WORLD JONES MADE Dick
A WORLD OF DIFFERENCE Conquest
WORLD OF GOL Charles
WORLD OF IF Phillips
THE WORLD OF NULL A van Vogt
WORLD OF THE MASTERMINDS Williams
WORLD OF TOMORROW Zeigfried
WORLD OUT OF MIND McIntosh
THE WORLD SWAPPERS Brunner
THE WORLD THAT COULDN'T BE Gold
THE WORLD THAT NEVER WAS Zeigfried
WORLD WITHOUT MEN Maine
WORLD WITHOUT WOMEN Keene and Pruyn
WORLDS APART McIntosh
WORLDS AT WAR Rayer
WORLD'S BEST SCIENCE FICTION: 1965 Wollheim and Carr
THE WORLDS OF CLIFFORD SIMAK Simak
WORLDS OF THE IMPERIUM Laumer
WORLDS OF TOMORROW Derleth
WORLDS OF WHEN Conklin
WORLDS TO CONQUER Statten
WORLDS WITHIN Phillips
WORLDS WITHOUT END Simak

THE WORM OUROBOROS Eddison

X Sudak
THE X MACHINE Muller
THE "X" PEOPLE Brack

YEAR OF CONSENT Crossen
THE YEAR OF THE MIRACLE Hume
YEAR 2018 Blish
THE YELLOW PLANET Brown
YONDER Beaumont
YOU CAN'T HANG THE DEAD Carroll
YOU SANE MEN Janifer
YOUR SINS AND MINE Caldwell
YOUTH MADNESS Coblentz

Z FORMATION Shaw
ZACHERLEY'S MIDNIGHT SNACKS Zacherley
ZACHERLEY'S VULTURE STEW Zacherley
ZENITH-D Lorraine
ZERO FIELD Hunt
ZERO HOUR Statten
ZERO MINUS X Zeigfried
ZERO POINT LePage
ZHORANI Maras

SCIENCE FICTION

An Arno Press Collection

FICTION

About, Edmond. **The Man with the Broken Ear.** 1872

Allen, Grant. **The British Barbarians:** A Hill-Top Novel. 1895

Arnold, Edwin L. **Lieut. Gullivar Jones:** His Vacation. 1905

Ash, Fenton. **A Trip to Mars.** 1909

Aubrey, Frank. **A Queen of Atlantis.** 1899

Bargone, Charles (Claude Farrere, pseud.). **Useless Hands.** [1926]

Beale, Charles Willing. **The Secret of the Earth.** 1899

Bell, Eric Temple (John Taine, pseud.). **Before the Dawn.** 1934

Benson, Robert Hugh. **Lord of the World.** 1908

Beresford, J. D. **The Hampdenshire Wonder.** 1911

Bradshaw, William R. **The Goddess of Atvatabar.** 1892

Capek, Karel. **Krakatit.** 1925

Chambers, Robert W. **The Gay Rebellion.** 1913

Colomb, P. et al. **The Great War of 189—.** 1893

Cook, William Wallace. **Adrift in the Unknown.** n.d.

Cummings, Ray. **The Man Who Mastered Time.** 1929

[DeMille, James]. **A Strange Manuscript Found in a Copper Cylinder.** 1888

Dixon, Thomas. **The Fall of a Nation:** A Sequel to the Birth of a Nation. 1916

England, George Allan. **The Golden Blight.** 1916

Fawcett, E. Douglas. **Hartmann the Anarchist.** 1893

Flammarion, Camille. **Omega:** The Last Days of the World. 1894

Grant, Robert et al. **The King's Men:** A Tale of To-Morrow. 1884

Grautoff, Ferdinand Heinrich (Parabellum, pseud.). **Banzai!** 1909

Graves, C. L. and E. V. Lucas. **The War of the Wenuses.** 1898

Greer, Tom. **A Modern Daedalus.** [1887]

Griffith, George. **A Honeymoon in Space.** 1901

Grousset, Paschal (A. Laurie, pseud.). **The Conquest of the Moon.** 1894

Haggard, H. Rider. **When the World Shook.** 1919

Hernaman-Johnson, F. **The Polyphemes.** 1906

Hyne, C. J. Cutcliffe. **Empire of the World.** [1910]

In The Future. [1875]

Jane, Fred T. **The Violet Flame.** 1899

Jefferies, Richard. **After London; Or, Wild England.** 1885

Le Queux, William. **The Great White Queen.** [1896]

London, Jack. **The Scarlet Plague.** 1915

Mitchell, John Ames. **Drowsy.** 1917

Morris, Ralph. **The Life and Astonishing Adventures of John Daniel.** 1751

Newcomb, Simon. **His Wisdom The Defender:** A Story. 1900

Paine, Albert Bigelow. **The Great White Way.** 1901

Pendray, Edward (Gawain Edwards, pseud.). **The Earth-Tube.** 1929

Reginald, R. and Douglas Menville. **Ancestral Voices:** An Anthology of Early Science Fiction. 1974

Russell, W. Clark. **The Frozen Pirate.** 2 vols. in 1. 1887

Shiel, M. P. **The Lord of the Sea.** 1901

Symmes, John Cleaves (Captain Adam Seaborn, pseud.). **Symzonia.** 1820

Train, Arthur and Robert W. Wood. **The Man Who Rocked the Earth.** 1915

Waterloo, Stanley. **The Story of Ab:** A Tale of the Time of the Cave Man. 1903

White, Stewart E. and Samuel H. Adams. **The Mystery.** 1907

Wicks, Mark. **To Mars Via the Moon.** 1911

Wright, Sydney Fowler. **Deluge: A Romance** *and* **Dawn.** 2 vols. in 1. 1928/1929

SCIENCE FICTION

NON-FICTION:
Including Bibliographies,
Checklists and Literary Criticism

Aldiss, Brian and Harry Harrison. **SF Horizons.** 2 vols. in 1. 1964/1965

Amis, Kingsley. **New Maps of Hell.** 1960

Barnes, Myra. **Linguistics and Languages in Science Fiction-Fantasy.** 1974

Cockcroft, T. G. L. **Index to the Weird Fiction Magazines.** 2 vols. in 1 1962/1964

Cole, W. R. **A Checklist of Science-Fiction Anthologies.** 1964

Crawford, Joseph H. et al. **"333": A Bibliography of the Science-Fantasy Novel.** 1953

Day, Bradford M. **The Checklist of Fantastic Literature in Paperbound Books.** 1965

Day, Bradford M. **The Supplemental Checklist of Fantastic Literature.** 1963

Gove, Philip Babcock. **The Imaginary Voyage in Prose Fiction.** 1941

Green, Roger Lancelyn. **Into Other Worlds:** Space-Flight in Fiction, From Lucian to Lewis. 1958

Menville, Douglas. **A Historical and Critical Survey of the Science Fiction Film.** 1974

Reginald, R. **Contemporary Science Fiction Authors,** First Edition. 1970

Samuelson, David. **Visions of Tomorow:** Six Journeys from Outer to Inner Space. 1974